Hypernatural

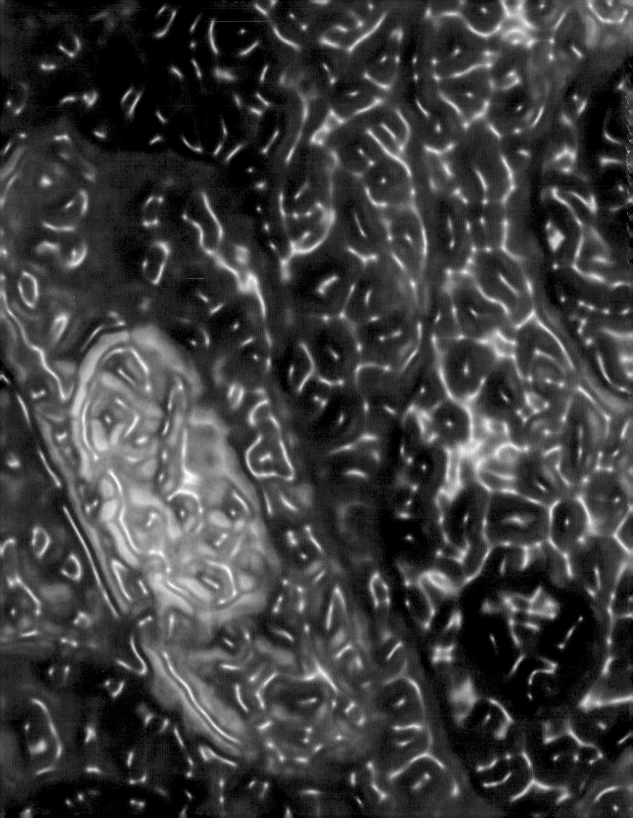

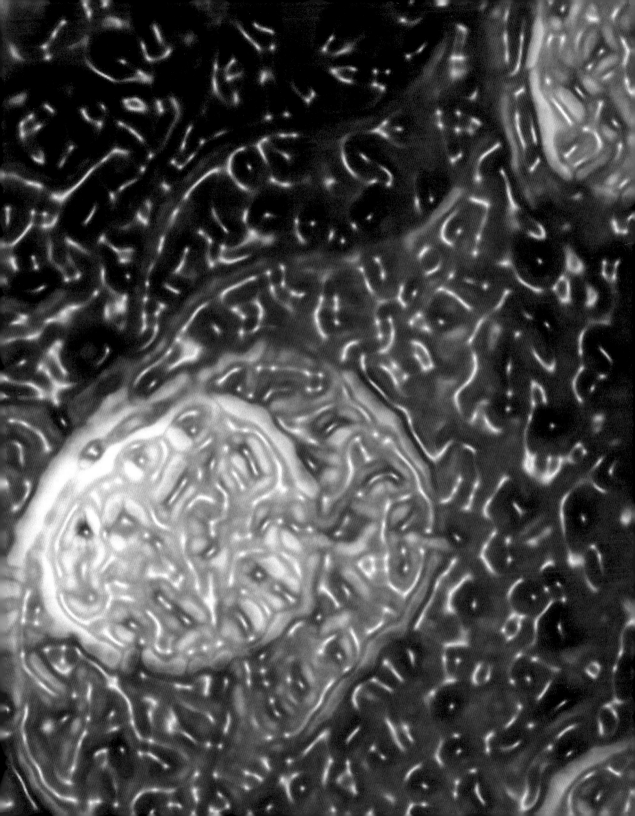

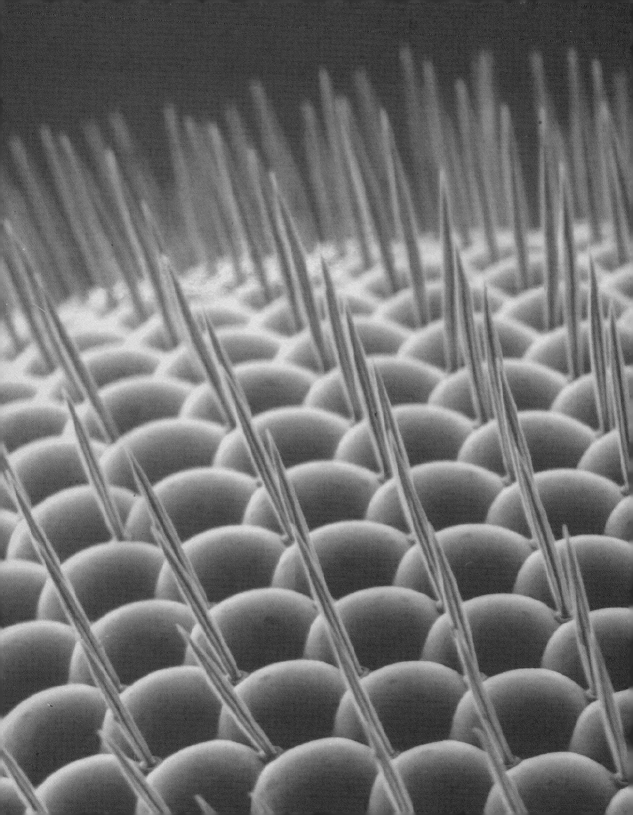

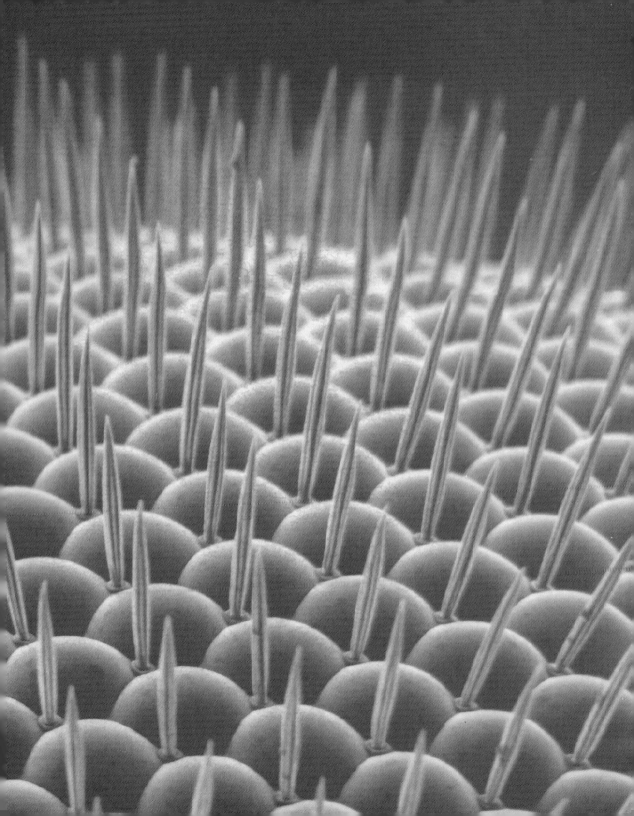

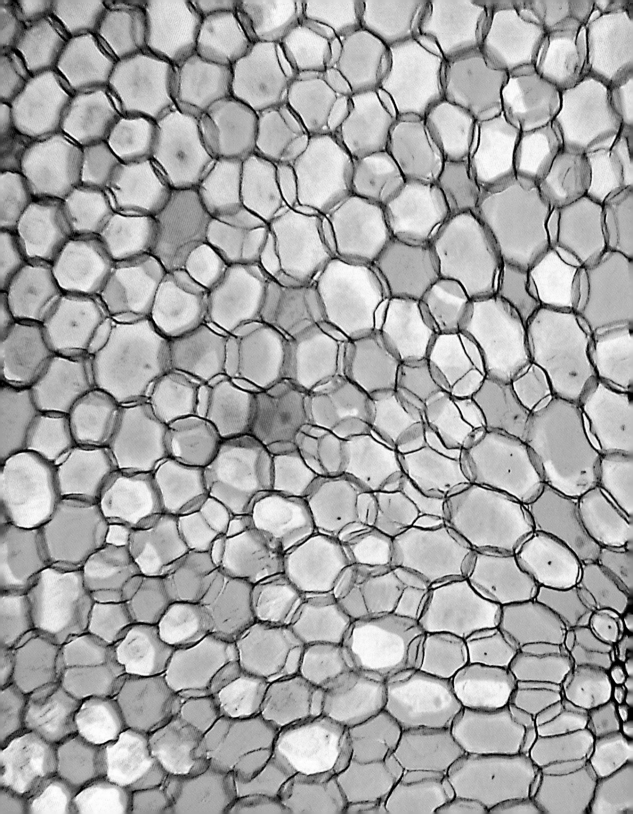

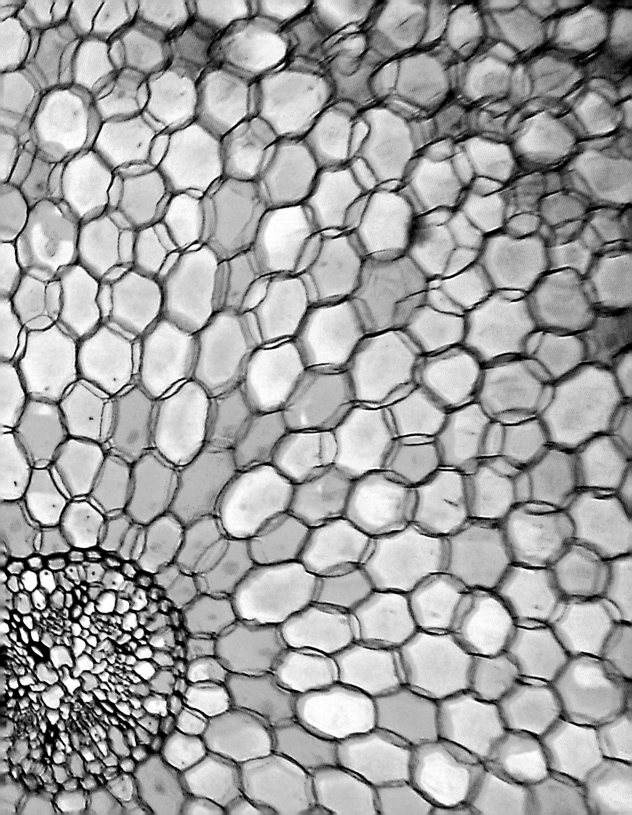

Architecture Briefs is a Princeton Architectural Press series
that addresses a variety of single topics of interest to architecture
students and professionals. Field-specific and technical information,
ranging from hand-drawn to digital methods, is presented in
a user-friendly manner alongside basics of architectural thought,
design, and construction. The series familiarizes readers with
the concepts and skills necessary to successfully translate ideas
into built form.

Also in the Architecture Briefs series:

Architectural Lighting
Designing with Light and Space
Hervé Descottes, Cecilia E. Ramos · 978-1-56898-938-9

Architectural Photography the Digital Way
Gerry Kopelow · 978-1-56898-697-5

Building Envelopes
An Integrated Approach
Jenny Lovell · 978-1-56898-818-4

Digital Fabrications
Architectural and Material Techniques
Lisa Iwamoto · 978-1-56898-790-3

Ethics for Architects
50 Dilemmas of Professional Practice
Thomas Fisher · 978-1-56898-946-4

Material Strategies
Innovative Applications in Architecture
Blaine Brownell · 978-1-56898-986-0

Model Making
Megan Werner · 978-1-56898-870-2

Old Buildings, New Designs
Architectural Transformations
Charles Bloszies · 978-1-61689-035-3

Philosophy for Architects
Branko Mitrović · 978-1-56898-994-5

Sustainable Design
A Critical Guide
David Bergman · 978-1-56898-941-9

Urban Composition
Designing Community through Urban Design
Mark Childs · 978-1-61689-052-0

Writing about Architecture
Mastering the Language of Buildings and Cities
Alexandra Lange · 978-1-61689-053-7

Blaine Brownell
and Marc Swackhamer

Hyper-
natural

Architecture's
New Relationship
with Nature

Princeton Architectural Press · New York

Published by:
Princeton Architectural Press
37 East 7th Street
New York, New York 10003
www.papress.com

Editor: Meredith Baber
Designer: Benjamin English

Special thanks to:
Sara Bader, Nicola Bednarek Brower, Janet Behning, Erin Cain,
Megan Carey, Carina Cha, Andrea Chlad, Barbara Darko,
Russell Fernandez, Jan Cigliano Hartman, Jan Haux, Mia Johnson,
Diane Levinson, Jennifer Lippert, Emily Malinowski,
Katharine Myers, Jaime Nelson, Rob Shaeffer, Sara Stemen,
Marielle Suba, Kaymar Thomas, Paul Wagner, Joseph Weston,
and Janet Wong of Princeton Architectural Press
—Kevin C. Lippert, publisher

Library of Congress Cataloging-in-Publication Data:
Brownell, Blaine Erickson, 1970– author.
Hypernatural : architecture's new relationship with nature /
Blaine Brownell and Marc Swackhamer.—First edition.
    pages cm.—(Architecture briefs)
Includes bibliographical references and index.
ISBN 978-1-61689-272-2 (alk. paper)
1. Architecture—Environmental aspects. 2. Architecture and
technology. 3. Nature (Aesthetics) I. Swackhamer, Marc, 1970–
author. II. Title.
NA2542.35.B79 2015
720.1′08—dc23   2014025559

To Heather, Connie, Blaine,
Maeve, Davis, and Enna

Foreword

All the forms that emerge from the processes of nature are intricately related. The forms of humans and other living species, the physical forms of the earth's surface, and the atmosphere—these forms regularly interact with each other and with their local environment. In doing so, they modify that environment, which in turn may undergo reactive changes to induce further modifications. The forms of the land, the ocean, and the atmosphere are dynamic three-dimensional patterns produced by the continuous physical processes of the natural world, and they are constantly being broken down and renewed. Biological forms, too, persist through multiple generations, but are never exactly the same from one generation to the next; they may exhibit significant changes over extended periods in response to changes in their environments. Humans, like all the species of the world, have been formed by nature and exist within nature. Knowledge exists in and is transmitted by culture, and human practices manifest that knowledge in the material forms of architecture. Culture acts to transmit complex social and ecologically contextual rules for material practices between local populations and through time.

The emergence of the modern human biological form cannot be separated from the development of human culture; the two have always been and continue to be interlocked in a coevolutionary process. From this perspective, culture does not stand outside of or beyond nature but is, rather, strongly coupled to it. Cultural evolution and the production of architecture coevolve with the natural systems of the world: all the works of humans are "natural," and in making the artifacts of civilization over the last ten thousand years we have changed nature. The understanding of the natural world—the very conception of nature—is culturally produced. This understanding has been subject to many changes throughout the evolution of the many different societies in the history of civilization.

As mutations to the known forms of organisms occur naturally, so too do small innovations. Theoretical "errors" and design mutations have driven the historical evolution of architecture from ancient material constructions to the built forms of the contemporary world. Culture evolves; it is a system of *descent with modification*, in which social and ecological forces determine which cultural variants are transmitted through time. Two of the most significant differences between biological and cultural evolution are the exponential growth in the acceleration of quantities and modalities of information transmission, and the *regime of selection* of forms that survive to pass on their genes to their descendants. Information transmission has been an essential characteristic of human culture since anatomically modern humans evolved from the great apes. The transmission of information of material practices and architectural forms has been accelerated exponentially several times, with the sequential emergence of large trading networks, mathematical notation, writing and drawing systems, printing, shipping, and worldwide navigation.

Humans are unique among species in that we have spread and proliferated through all climatic and ecological systems by means of cultural adaptations and innovations, changing the environment to suit us, whereas all other species have changed themselves by biological adaptations to variations in the environment. Biological adaption of species is strongly correlated to and constrained by the carrying capacity of the ecological system within which they exist. By contrast, successive waves of cultural innovations throughout the short history of modern humans have enabled the growth of populations, each energy and technological transition extracting more from the same resources while making more resources available and, in doing so, reconfiguring the carrying capacity to ever higher numbers. However, population growth increases the complexity of societies as well as the use of ecological, energy, and material resources, which in turn drives the need for a new wave of cultural innovations. When population growth is exponential the rate of cultural evolution is accelerated, and the environmental changes induced by humans also accelerate. It is widely thought that when steady, linear growth transitions to superlinear or unconstrained growth, the pace of life accelerates, and successive waves of innovations are required more and more frequently. In the natural world, change is normal, but its intricate choreography is now further accelerated and perturbed by human activities. Global climate change is upon us, and its effects will be local and regional—more energy trapped in volatile weather systems produces unprecedented behavior and unpredictable consequences. Similarly, the emergent behavior of local economies and cultures, now connected and interlinked globally, are substantially reconfigured. It is clear that the world is within the horizon of a systemic change and that transitions through multiple critical thresholds will cascade through all the systems of nature and civilization.

The conceptual apparatus of human architecture has always given a central role to the relations of humankind and nature. A large body of scientific work over the last century has had a profound impact on our understanding of the physics and processes of the natural world. The current engagement of both architectural practice and theoretical discourse with nature is a reflection of the availability of new modes of imaging the intricate and the very small, of computational simulations of evolution, morphogenesis, and behavior, and of the increasingly broad acceptance that all the living and nonliving forms of the world emerge from the dynamic processes of nature. It has been widely remarked that biology was the leading scientific discipline of the twentieth century, and it is evident that it remains close to the center of scientific discourse in the early twenty-first century. The cultural parameters of contemporary cultural fascination with a new understanding of nature and of natural forms are driving architectural innovations. New working methods of architectural design and production are rapidly spreading through architectural and engineering practices, having already revised the world of manufacturing and construction. New strategies for design and production are evident: strategies derived from natural forms and systems, from their material properties and metabolisms, and from their adaptive response to changes in their environment. Computationally driven design and production processes are enabling the fabrication of architectural forms that exhibit complex responsive behavior, and perhaps even real intelligence. New architectural and infrastructural forms are emerging and will proliferate across the world as constructed material artifacts that are more closely and symbiotically related to the ecological systems and processes of the natural world.

In the intricately connected world today there are multiple ways to design and produce architectures that are informed by nature, and as the ideas and

processes hybridize and spread around the world, they are transitioning through a critical threshold in culture into the "hypernatural" that is the subject of this book. Hypernatural is conventionally defined as a state of existing in nature or being formed by nature—however, in contemporary discourses it is increasingly used to suggest a state of being that extends beyond "wild" nature, in which the boundary between the natural and the artificial is ambiguous and indeterminate. This book sets out a cartography of the historical and current changes in the relationship between the societal understanding of the natural world, the material practices and technologies, and the production of architecture. The projects within the book exhibit a wide variety of ideas and works that have arisen from these changes. It makes a significant contribution to this domain, and I am delighted to be associated with it.

— Michael Weinstock

Introduction

[Werner] Sombart pointed out, in a long list of contrasting productions and inventions, that the clue to modern technology was the displacement of the organic and the living by the artificial and the mechanical. Within technology itself this process, in many departments, is being reversed: we are returning to the organic; at all events, we no longer regard the mechanical as all-embracing and all-sufficient.

— Lewis Mumford, *Technics and Civilization*, 1934

The ultimate aim of technology is not antinatural; it is *hypernatural*. It involves working directly with natural forces and processes—rather than against them—in order to amplify, extend, or exceed natural capacities. This approach characterizes many fields of human industry today, including science, engineering, architecture, and art, which are infused with a growing enthusiasm and reverence for nature. Scientists craft photosynthetic cells made from trees, engineers encapsulate stratified clouds within buildings, architects design structures that simulate the phototropic behavior of plants, and artists grow rooms made of mineral crystals. Fig. 1 In both academia and practice, the conviction that nature holds the keys to the advancement of technology and design is now a primary motivator. Moreover, endeavors guided by a sophisticated knowledge of natural systems have the potential to counteract the increasing fragility and degradation of the natural environment.

To be certain, humanity has used technology to wreak havoc on nature. We have employed tools and methods to establish our place as the dominant species on the planet, leaving in our wake environmental devastation, biodiversity loss, pervasive pollution, and a transformed global climate. This negligent practice must cease for many reasons—not the least of which is our own future survival. However, we err when we blame technology for this outcome, for technology is merely a vehicle—albeit a powerful one. The notions that technology embodies inherently antinatural principles or that it is a domain squarely under the control of human operations are both inaccurate and dangerous presumptions, for they limit the full potential of technology as a creative force that can benefit us as well as the planet.

Using the built environment as a primary focus of concern, this book intends to demonstrate this

positive capacity of technology. It also aspires to establish a new discourse on architecture's relationship with the natural world, exemplified by innovative approaches that architects and designers now use to integrate nature and human technology in profound ways. We hope that the articulation of a new conceptual framework will not only provide readers with a more insightful comprehension of this relationship but also inspire abundant innovative opportunities in future design.

A Changing Paradigm

Over the course of history humanity's increased dominion over—and apparent separation from—the natural environment has resulted in a binary view of the physical world: one realm designed by and for humans and another outside our influence. This dichotomy has become increasingly rigid over the millennia, as humans first sought stability and protection apart from the dangerous wilds—and eventually established control over natural resources and systems, manipulating and processing them far beyond their original states. The Industrial Revolution—the juggernaut of human-built machines demonstrating the intoxicating potential of mass production at tremendous environmental cost—was the historic milestone that has come to symbolize technology's complete disassociation from nature. The unassailable forces of industry have since propelled the exponential growth of cities and human development throughout the globe, resulting in the unprecedented coverage of the earth's surface with human-engineered environments that support an accelerating urban population.

However, increasing awareness of the near-total influence of human activity on the planet has engendered two recent, profound shifts in thinking. The first is obvious: the massive extent of human operations and swift decline of natural resources, wilderness, and unadulterated landscapes have resulted in a newfound appreciation for the natural world. This realization is evident in the growing importance of fields such as sustainability, biophilia, and biomimicry, which seek to undo the damage caused by excessive and polluting human operations.[1] The second shift is less apparent yet no less significant: the intensified scrutiny of natural and

1. Bloom, by DOSU Studio
Architecture, Los Angeles,
California, 2012

2. Atomic force micrograph showing
self-assembled molecules of two different
materials that form a tunable surface

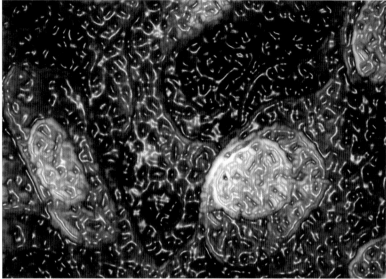

human-based processes has revealed that they are more similar than previously thought. This is partly due to the fact that more advanced human creations—such as a city, financial market, or the Internet—tend to resemble the inherent complexities and behaviors of natural systems, and must adhere to natural principles in order to endure. It is also attributable to an emerging outlook that positions humanity—and by association its activities—as part of the natural world, rather than separate from it.

The Nature of Technology, the Technology of Nature

These views become self-evident with a broader assessment of technology and nature. On the one hand, technology may be seen as a natural phenomenon. As early as the mid-nineteenth century, scholars have suggested that technology adheres to similar evolutionary principles as natural organisms. In his 1863 essay "Darwin among the Machines," Samuel Butler argued that human technologies might be viewed as a kind of "mechanical life," with growing autonomy and influence over human affairs.[2] Sociologist S. Colum Gilfillan, zoologist Bashford Dean, and biologist Niles Eldredge have chronicled the development of human technologies—such as naval architecture, military armaments, and musical instruments, respectively—according to natural principles of evolutionary development. In 1994 author Kevin Kelly demonstrated the extent to which the mechanical and biological worlds are becoming fused in *Out of Control*—referencing examples such as self-assembling robots that act like living cells or computational machines constructed out of *E. coli* bacteria.[3] Fig. 2 More recently, in *The Nature of Technology*, economist W. Brian Arthur set out to establish a new theory of technology, which is grounded in evolutionary thinking.[4]

On the other hand, nature can be seen as a technological force. A common assumption is that technology is the exclusive realm of *Homo sapiens*; however, science indicates otherwise. The study of ethology, which concerns animal behaviors, is replete with examples of animal-fabricated tools—from chimpanzees' use of stones for grinding nuts to elephants' employment of branches to swat flies. Once our sphere of technology is appropriately broadened to include any organism's construction of shelter and manipulation of the environment, the examples multiply beyond count—including every beaver dam, beehive, bird's nest, or hermit crab refuge. Seen in this way, technology is an instrument of life and has

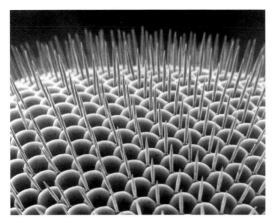

been utilized for millions of years by organisms of varying levels of evolutionary development.

An even broader interpretation of technology exists when we expand the definition to include corporeal agency. After all, nature exhibits a nearly endless supply of technologies represented by the organs, appendages, and processes employed by living creatures to gain natural advantage in the evolutionary chain. For example, the mind-numbing venom of the parasitic wasp, the protective carapace of the tortoise, or the nocturnal echolocation of the bat may all be considered technologies that have evolved as tools of survival in living organisms. In *What Technology Wants*, Kelly makes a case for nature's technological evolution with the example of the eye, the remarkable "biological camera" that developed multiple times in completely separate species: "Neither Darwin nor his critics appreciated the fact that the cameralike eye evolved not just once—miracle though it may seem—but six times over the course of life on Earth."[5] Fig. 3

Technology vs. Design, Design vs. Beauty
In most disciplines, technology and design are considered separate and distinct concerns. However, common definitions of the terms—"the practical application of knowledge" (technology) and "the art or action of conceiving" (design)—are similar in that they both describe processes of creative implementation.[6] Moreover, seen through a more comprehensive natural lens, technology and design become inseparable. We can certainly appreciate the

design of a natural technology like the leaf window of the *fenestraria* plant, which focuses and magnifies sunlight used for photosynthesis—as much as we can marvel at the technology of a natural design like the male peacock's vivid plumage, which serves to attract female mates as a necessary step toward ensuring the propagation of the species. Fig. 4 In these and other examples of natural agency—including the tools and structures devised by other animal species—it is impossible to draw a line between technology and design, for they are one and the same.

Like the peacock's polychromatic feathers, natural designs are often aptly described as beautiful. Humans exhibit a strong attraction to beauty in the physical environment—thus beauty is often promoted as an objective of design. "Every business should be completely concerned with beauty—it is, after all, a collective human need," says designer Karim Rashid.[7] However, establishing beauty as an objective for design is a precarious act, for beauty is a subjective criterion that is limited by existing standards and mores. Nature is beautiful and ugly, welcoming and frightening. The blood-sucking proboscis of the mosquito and the devastating, debris-filled tornado cloud are rarely considered beautiful, yet they are both remarkable natural phenomena that merit respect and further study. Hypernatural designs do not aim to be beautiful—although they may result in alluring outcomes or exhibit underlying systems or processes that are beautiful. Rather, the hypernatural approach precipitates transformation, novelty, and mutation,

in both technology and design, generating aesthetic results that may be uncanny, sublime, or otherwise challenging to evaluate based on status quo models.

Hypernatural Architecture

Natural organisms aim to make the world hypernatural—not in the improbable sense of being better than nature but in manifesting the *next nature*, a state that transcends current archetypes and provides a more advantageous set of circumstances. From a deterministic standpoint, one could describe hypernature as the very aim of evolution itself—although evolution is a complex, messy process of random occurrences that does not always generate obvious improvements over existing traits. According to designers Koert Van Mensvoort and Hendrik-Jan Grievink, "hypernature brings us 'natural' experiences that could not exist without the human hand, but can be appreciated nonetheless."[8] We argue that this definition should be expanded to include all life, for the manipulation of nature is not limited to human influence. For example, just as the human-domesticated cow may be considered hypernatural, so might the ant-domesticated—and similarly behaviorally transformed—aphid.

Hypernature also includes the modification of nonliving matter by living organisms for the purposes of reshaping their physical environments. The termite mound, for instance, is simultaneously part of the natural landscape as well as a form of animal architecture. Fig. 5 Humans consider the mound to be completely natural, yet the structure augments

the preexisting landscape, changing it in a way that directly benefits the activities of the termite colony. The *termitaria* can therefore be said to transcend the conditions of its extant context in a way that enables its inhabitants not merely to survive but to flourish. In this sense the termite mound and human structures are no different. Although this perspective contradicts the age-old notion that human creations are inherently nonnatural, the growing acknowledgment that a deeper connection exists between so-called human and natural domains has facilitated the pursuit of new opportunities as well as the achievement of unprecedented outcomes in architecture and other creative disciplines.

Outlined in this book are a diversity of approaches to the research, development, and fabrication of projects focused on uncovering new relationships between the born and the made. The featured designers maintain refreshingly unconventional, radical definitions of nature. Rather than revere it as a bucolic, idealized condition, they attempt to expose nature holistically—including its most unpleasant, undignified, even threatening states. These architects, artists, and engineers consider the death and decay of their work as seriously as they consider its design and construction. They speculate on how buildings can dynamically evolve over the course of a day, season, or year, in response to violent change. They relish in the messy complexity that grows out of a simple set of rules, set into motion with no assurance as to the effectiveness of their outcome. Decay, change, and unpredictability: these are three words to which architects have commonly exhibited resistance, but to which hypernatural designers enthusiastically flock.

Nature resists conventional design processes primarily because it resists control. Much of the work presented here results from a deliberate effort on the part of its authors to relinquish dominance over their work. Traditionally, architects have thrived on control—the more control they have over a project, the better the building, so the adage goes. However, hypernatural architects deliberately resituate control, often to the predesign phase of a project, where they set up the conditions for work to unfold, organically and unpredictably. An identified natural force then assumes control of the work, exerting its authorial will in ways that are never the same twice. In such a process one does not so much control nature, or even imitate it, as partner with it.

Additionally, craft is vitally important in these case studies, but in a different way than we typically consider it. Like control, the crafting of work occurs before its conception, during its predesign. It is the precision with which nature is set into motion, with which problems are strategically framed, and with which the decay of work is carefully considered. For example, in Andrew Kudless's *Chrysalis (III)* project, a dynamic digital armature anticipates the dense packing of barnacle-like cells across a surface. Fig. 6 While the digital system conceived to organize and array those cells is crafted with precision, the actual arrangement of cells on the surface, with their variations in size, density, shape, and orientation, are all dependent on forces that lie outside the hand of the designer. Final appearance is not curated or crafted in a traditional way (through an aesthetic assessment or comparison to a proportioning system). Similarly, Philip Beesley's *Radiant Soil* project is a precisely well-crafted, biotechnical system of glass vessels, metallic fronds, and networks of tubing and wiring. Fig. 7 However, the project continually changes in response to occupant movement. So the project never looks, smells, or feels the same. It is precision-crafted in its ability to change, while craft, as it refers to a single, unchanging, curated detail, is of little concern.

An entirely different set of metrics for assessing the elegance, craftsmanship, and beauty of work is emerging from hypernatural research. It is not just a new kind of architecture that is being produced but also an entirely new collection of ways to work, discuss, and critique.

Hypernatural Approaches

When architects, designers, or scientists consider working with nature, they tend to pursue one of two approaches: representation or engagement. Representation is composed of the translation of natural forms or behaviors into new materials or systems. Terms like organic architecture and biomimicry apply here.[9] This approach includes examples such as floral motifs carved into stone for the purposes of ornamentation, as well as synthetic polymers that emulate the insoluble adhesion of mussel byssal threads. In both cases there is a measurable distinction between the natural source and the representation it has inspired. Unlike representation, engagement involves direct interaction with natural substances—including living organisms—to create new designs. Terms like *geodesign* and *bioengineering* are relevant here.[10] This approach consists of examples like bio bricks made by the calcifying processes of bacteria or bio-photovoltaics that employ living algae to harness solar energy. In both instances there is a clear blurring of natural processes and human-initiated purpose, and the outcome may be less predictable than in works of representation.

Although this dichotomy seems clear, it has notable limitations. First, it creates a hard line between works that simply model nature versus those that

9. *Seizure*, by Roger
Hiorns, Yorkshire,
United Kingdom, 2008

10. *Windswept*, by Charles
Sowers, San Francisco,
California, 2012

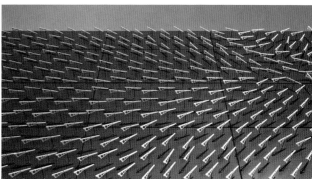

actually interact with it. The suggestion is that one
must decide between a remote, intellectual stance
versus a hands-on, pragmatic one. In reality there
is no distinct barrier between these methods, and
designers often combine or blend approaches as
needed. Second, this paradigm reinforces a distinction
between the natural and the artificial: the assumption is that one either represents nature in artificial
materials or combines natural and artificial materials.
However, this duality is largely mythical and inhibits
an appreciation for the shared qualities, capabilities,
or aspirations between the so-called natural and
human domains.

A survey of the projects included in this book
invites consideration of another set of approaches
in the spirit of producing hypernatural work. Such
methods combine representation and engagement,
and de-emphasize the natural-artificial dichotomy
that can interfere with the achievement of innovative
design. Specifically, three distinct terms generally
serve to categorize designers' and architects' various
approaches to working hypernaturally: *properties*,
processes, and *phenomena*. In each case, a fundamental transformation occurs that transcends
common practice.

Properties include the inherent structure, chemistry, and fundamental makeup of things. Architects
might use this approach when devising a finite structure or assembly based on natural elements, patterns,
or forces. For example, the *Water Cathedral* by
GUN Architects utilizes suspended, water-dispensing
fabric cones whose geometry adheres to the same
fluid dynamics principles that govern the formation

of stalactites and icicles. Fig. 8 Here the transformation
occurs during the design process, as natural logic is
harnessed to create a novel type of sheltering surface.

Processes concern the empowerment of natural
agency in construction. Designers employ this method
like scientists, establishing the materials and framework for an experiment that they subsequently set into
motion. An example is *Seizure*, an interior installation
that Roger Hiorns created by submerging an empty
apartment in a mineral bath for several weeks, allowing copper sulfate crystals to precipitate on all the
existing surfaces. Fig. 9 In this case the transformation
takes place during construction—with nature-driven
procedures as the principal focus.

Phenomena describe responsive, interactive, or
transformational capabilities in design. Here architects create circumstantial works that change based
on contextual or other stimuli akin to the movements
of living creatures or fluctuating weather patterns.
An example is Charles Sowers's *Windswept*, a wind-
responsive surface composed of an array of small,
delicately balanced weather vanes that reveal the
complex, microscaled interactions of airflow against
a building envelope. Fig. 10 Here the transformation
occurs postconstruction on a continual and fluctuating
basis as it relates to the local climate.

Designing with Life
Although the approaches of properties, processes,
and phenomena may be applied to a wide variety of
natural science fields, the life sciences merit particular
attention, given the characteristic complexity, growth,
and reproductive capacity of biological organisms.

11. *Silk Pavilion*, by the Mediated Matter
group, Massachusetts Institute of Technology,
Cambridge, Massachusetts, 2013

12. ICD/ITKE Research Pavilion, by
Achim Menges and Jan Knippers,
Stuttgart, Germany, 2012

13. Stratus Project,
by RVTR, Ann Arbor,
Michigan, 2011

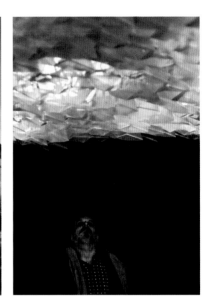

Architects pursuing life science–based work may therefore adopt a specific set of methods—*behavioral*, *genetic*, and *epigenetic*—related to designing with biology.

Behavioral projects typically consider biology before construction. In this approach, design work occurs most intensively during the setup of the project, allowing for its specific characteristics to unfold as a direct result of a biological behavior. For example, Neri Oxman's *Silk Pavilion* leverages knowledge of silkworms, producing an armature before the construction of the project, which the caterpillars later populate and on which they cast their silk in particular patterns. Fig. 11 The project's characteristics and appearance are an outcome of strategies set into motion before the project is actually fabricated. These projects are dependent on the behavior of an organism in relationship to a system conceived of prior to construction by the architect.

Genetic projects engage with biology during construction. Genes, of course, are biological building blocks that carry with them all the information necessary for passing traits from one generation of organisms to another. They are responsible for the development and growth of an organism from conception to birth. After birth, an organism's characteristics are dependent on a combination of genetic information (nature) and environmental fluctuation (nurture). Genetic projects are those that emulate a growth pattern or other genetically informed system during their construction. For example, the ICD/ITKE Research Pavilion by Achim Menges and Jan Knippers leverages an in-depth understanding of lobster shells and their layered fibrous structure to inform a pattern of woven carbon fiber thread on its skin. Fig. 12 Genetic information about how the thread is to be woven is embedded in a tool path dictating the movement of a robotic arm. Nature exclusively informs the outcome of a genetic project. After construction, a genetic project is typically static and unchanging.

Epigenetic projects engage with biology after construction. *Epigenetic* simply refers to a biological characteristic that results from an external force as opposed to an internal (or genetic) force. Epigenetic projects dynamically change after a building is constructed, in response to particular site forces, like wind, precipitation, or temperature, or in response to internal fluctuation, like changes in occupancy or movements of people. For example, the Stratus Project by RVTR is a dynamic interior building skin with dynamic cells that open and close like fish gills, in response to quantities and movements of people to change the quality of air and light inside a space. Fig. 13 Just as biology reacts in real time to changes in its environment (e.g., goose bumps on the skin), epigenetic projects adapt to change through programmed logics (e.g., sensors and computers that monitor conditions) or through engineered materials that change their properties automatically (e.g., shape memory alloys or composites that deflect and bend with variations in temperature).

Explanation of the Book

Hypernatural is intended to address the changing relationship between the designed environment and the natural world as well as the opportunities that arise from this transformation. Written for a broad audience that includes architects, engineers, artists, scientists, and environmental enthusiasts, the book has three primary objectives: coherence, context, and application.

Recent decades have witnessed the increasing popularity of nature-focused movements, such as sustainability, biophilia, biomimicry, biodesign, and emergent design. Although overlaps exist, there is no common discourse that unites these areas of study. The book attempts to establish an inclusive and coherent framework that enables these and other nature-related movements to be more fully understood. The frame of reference that we employ is borrowed from the natural sciences—simplified into a set of seven chapters. These chapters are organized in a loose chronological order of planetary development starting with the domains that existed prior to life: the geosphere, atmosphere, and hydrosphere. Three subsequent chapters are devoted to life itself, subdivided according to micro- and macro-organisms (microbial), plant (botanical), and animal (zoological) biospheres. The final chapter concerns the noosphere—or domain of human thought—which we propose as a legitimate natural sphere worthy of consideration.

Many contemporary architects, scientists, and engineers are pursuing a specific nature-related agenda without extensive knowledge of each other's approaches or the historical influences that have shaped them. The second goal of the book is therefore to provide a broad context for a concise set of relevant technological, environmental, and social transformations that have occurred throughout human history.

Each chapter is subdivided into sections that address significant areas of concern, including historical background, material basis and behaviors, technologies, and design applications. Greater depth is provided with a project story that introduces each chapter, as well as a series of case studies of notable contemporary projects that conclude each chapter.

Throughout the book we evaluate the ways in which humanity's changing relationship with nature has transformed creative practice. Until now, the lack of a coherent framework has resulted in much confusion regarding nature-focused approaches to design. For example, a designer who grows a piece of furniture out of crystals in a mineral bath might be incorrectly described as pursuing a biomimetic agenda—however, this approach has less to do with biology or mimicry than with geology and design. In another example, concepts such as biomimicry and emergence are often considered recent trends, yet these approaches are evident throughout history. Thus the book also aims to clarify application methodology—as a way to both assess existing practices and provide a road map for the development of new approaches.

Today, architects and designers operate within an increasingly complex, volatile, and tightly interconnected world. Dwindling resources, eroding biodiversity, and chronic environmental health problems have inspired the design and construction communities to pursue a mission of environmental sustainability. Yet this worthy objective has largely been shaped by considerations of technology, policy, and professional practice without a concomitant investment in design. Unfortunately, status quo approaches to creating buildings and environments will not solve emerging problems or unlock new opportunities. The works included here are therefore intended to demonstrate the transformative potential of design, revealing its capacity to engage natural principles, systems, and phenomena in innovative ways. After all, nature is a repository of virtually limitless knowledge that awaits the curiosity of architects, engineers, and artists—particularly those with open minds—to discover new possibilities for fashioning the constructed environment. It is our aspiration that readers will be awakened to such newfound potential in their own work.

GEOSPHERE

Crystals form when molecules of a particular material (like salt) are placed in a solution where they incrementally merge until a visible cubic or triangular tessellated growth is formed. The process can happen in minutes or it can take thousands of years, but it always begins at an atomic level. The shape of an element's atoms determines the shape of its crystals. Crystal growth is called *nucleation*.[1] Unassisted nucleation occurs when crystals form exclusively in a given solution, without a sublattice to encourage their growth. Assisted nucleation, by contrast, occurs when crystals initially adhere to an already present sublattice, which catalyzes their growth in a specific shape and direction.

Through research into crystal growth, designer Tokujin Yoshioka has developed two prototype chairs that are grown out of the process of nucleation. One of the chairs, the *Venus Natural Crystal Chair*, is grown on a block of soft polyester approximating the shape of a chair in a solution where it is slowly layered, one crystal at a time (see pp 30–31). *Spider's Thread Chair* is similarly grown slowly over time, but in this case, crystals are encouraged to follow a path describing the outline of a chair that has first been defined by an assembly of stretched strings. While both projects are more discursive than functional, they offer new ways of considering fabrication, craft, and the role natural systems play in the design process. Yoshioka only sets up the circumstances under which fabrication of the chairs will unfold. He never prescribes exactly how the chairs will look or in what sequence they will be assembled. This is left up to the chemical properties of the crystals and the environment in which they are grown. The designer partners with these unpredictable natural forces, calling into question conventional notions of craft and authorial will. Yoshioka suggests that his design, "which is formed using the laws of nature and embodies a beauty born of coincidence, pushes the boundaries of creativity."[2]

If natural forces can participate in design outcomes, what are other unconventional, extra-designer considerations that might do the same? In work related to *Venus* and *Spider's Thread Chair*, Yoshioka speculates on this question. In *Swan Lake*, he captures the tonal vibrations of Pyotr Tchaikovsky's seminal work to produce a crystal "painting" that emerges slowly from music pulses in a crystal solution. This unassisted nucleation process takes nearly six months to complete. In *The Rose*, he leverages assisted nucleation to grow crystals on the outer surface of a rose, again, slowly over time, extending the pattern of metamorphosis encountered by the flower in its life cycle.

In all this work, focus is placed on the issue of authorial will—the hand of the designer is interrogated. The promise of Yoshioka's work, and others in this chapter, is that the designer becomes orchestrator, setting the stage for a complex array of forces and stimuli to influence project outcome. The work is more difficult to predict and highly varied from one iteration to the next, but also more tightly wedded to its context and acutely aware of subtle, situational variation. Nature provides the novelty.

Background

A common origin myth explains that the first human beings were made from clay. The Egyptian god Khnum, a ram-headed deity known as "The Great Potter," is said to have given life to humankind on his potter's wheel. The Qur'an tells a similar story in which Allah molds and breathes life into clay. Despite the fantastical nature of these accounts, science reinforces our physical connection with the earth. At least sixty chemical elements are found in the average human body, including silicon, oxygen, hydrogen, calcium, iron, and sodium—all primary ingredients of clay.[3] Moreover, a study conducted by Massachusetts General Hospital scientists revealed that montmorillonite clay may have been critical to the formation of life, because of its chemical support of the development of cell membranes.[4] Philosopher Manuel De Landa describes the "mineralization" of vertebrates in the formation of bone, a process that enabled a newfound freedom of movement.[5] A subsequent mineralization occurred in the form of human constructions—the earthen bricks and stone walls composed of the "urban exoskeleton" that appeared about eight millennia ago.[6] By regulating the movement of people and goods, this mineral structure "may be said to perform, for tightly packed populations of humans, the same function of motion control that our bones do in relation to our fleshy parts."[7] Thus, our relationship to the geosphere is characterized by movement as well as stasis, by freedom as well as constraint. Over time,

our attention has shifted from the products of mineralization to the process itself, as humans have become more attuned to mineral flows within the physical environment.

The cave is one of the archetypal birthplaces of architecture: a discovered volume of bedrock provided welcome shelter from the elements. As earthen building evolved, humans adopted additive as well as subtractive approaches to manipulating geological materials. Early structures of sun-dried clay and stone were load-bearing architecture connected directly to the land, and anticipated an increasingly layered *terra synthetica* of mineral urbanization. Fig. 1 In this way landscape suggested both context and resource—earth as either site or material for building. Kiln-fired brick and ceramic tile mimicked natural processes of metamorphic rock formation, chemically transforming earthen materials via intense heat. In the skilled hands of Roman engineers, earthen materials were made to span considerable horizontal distances. The masonry- or concrete-based arch, vault, and dome enabled the construction of fabricated caves for mineral enclosure. By the Middle Ages earthen architecture became increasingly immaterial, as seen in the soaring volumes of Gothic structures precariously supported by lacy stone filigree. Fig. 2

The gradual dematerialization of earthen building materials heralded the transition from the bearing wall to the structural frame. Lofty stone constructions eventually gave way to even thinner and taller skeletons of iron and steel, the geosphere-derived metals produced by the fires of industrial furnaces. The structural frame enabled additional freedoms: the liberation of the facade from its weight-supporting role and the free vertical movement of people and goods within multistory structures of unprecedented height. At the same time, the frame also created an identity crisis for the mineralized facade: once free from its original function of carrying a building, earthen masonry became dead weight. Despite this loss of purpose and encumbered application, stone and brick have remained enormously popular cladding materials because of their visual representation of strength and endurance. Clearly, people place a high value on the durable presence that masonry facades communicate, even if this is merely a superficial portrayal.

In recent times, additive manufacturing has ushered in yet another type of mineralization. Ceramics, metals, concretes, and plastics—geosphere-derived substances that contain the bulk of today's building materials—may all be 3-D printed directly from digital data. This newfound capability has facilitated the

Venus Chair

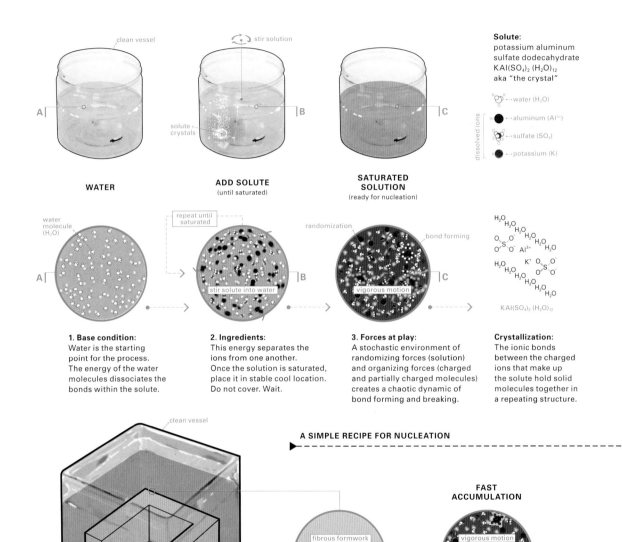

WATER

clean vessel

A|

ADD SOLUTE
(until saturated)

stir solution

solute crystals

B|

SATURATED SOLUTION
(ready for nucleation)

C|

Solute:
potassium aluminum sulfate dodecahydrate $KAl(SO_4)_2 (H_2O)_{12}$ aka "the crystal"

→ water (H_2O)
→ aluminum (Al^{3+})
→ sulfate (SO_4)
→ potassium (K)

dissolved ions

water molecule (H_2O)

A|

repeat until saturated

stir solute into water

B|

randomization

bond forming

vigorous motion

C|

H_2O H_2O H_2O
O S O^- H_2O H_2O
O^- O^- Al^{3+} H_2O
H_2O K^+ O S O^-
H_2O O^- O^-
H_2O H_2O
H_2O

$KAl(SO_4)_2 (H_2O)_{12}$

1. Base condition:
Water is the starting point for the process. The energy of the water molecules dissociates the bonds within the solute.

2. Ingredients:
This energy separates the ions from one another. Once the solution is saturated, place it in stable cool location. Do not cover. Wait.

3. Forces at play:
A stochastic environment of randomizing forces (solution) and organizing forces (charged and partially charged molecules) creates a chaotic dynamic of bond forming and breaking.

Crystallization:
The ionic bonds between the charged ions that make up the solute hold solid molecules together in a repeating structure.

clean vessel

A SIMPLE RECIPE FOR NUCLEATION

▶ -

FAST ACCUMULATION

C|

fibrous formwork

D^A|

vigorous motion

D^A|

polyethylene foam mold

SATURATED SOLUTION
(ready for nucleation)

4^A. Formwork:
A relatively stable surface (a foam mold) reduces the effects of randomization.

5^A. Mediated growth:
Nucleation is mediated on a determined surface. This increases the probability of bonding by holding molecules still. The rougher the surface the better the hold.

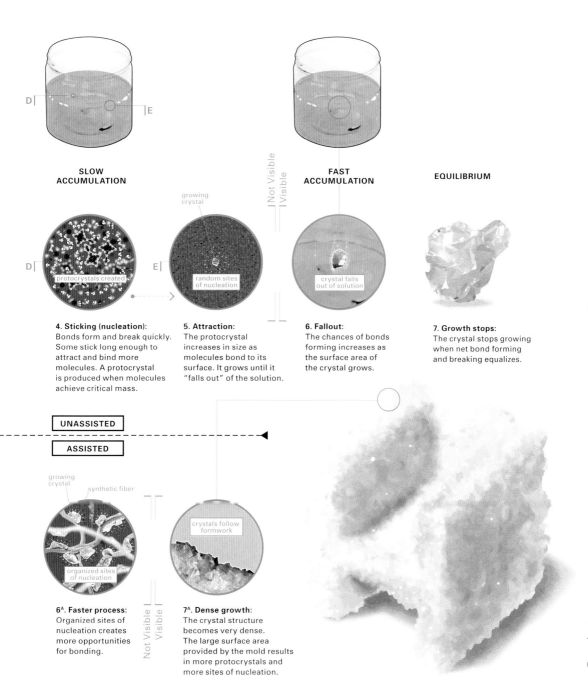

SLOW ACCUMULATION

FAST ACCUMULATION

EQUILIBRIUM

Not Visible | Visible

D | E

growing crystal

protocrystals created

random sites of nucleation

crystal falls out of solution

4. Sticking (nucleation):
Bonds form and break quickly. Some stick long enough to attract and bind more molecules. A protocrystal is produced when molecules achieve critical mass.

5. Attraction:
The protocrystal increases in size as molecules bond to its surface. It grows until it "falls out" of the solution.

6. Fallout:
The chances of bonds forming increases as the surface area of the crystal grows.

7. Growth stops:
The crystal stops growing when net bond forming and breaking equalizes.

UNASSISTED

ASSISTED

growing crystal

synthetic fiber

organized sites of nucleation

crystals follow formwork

Not Visible | Visible

6ᴬ. Faster process:
Organized sites of nucleation creates more opportunities for bonding.

7ᴬ. Dense growth:
The crystal structure becomes very dense. The large surface area provided by the mold results in more protocrystals and more sites of nucleation.

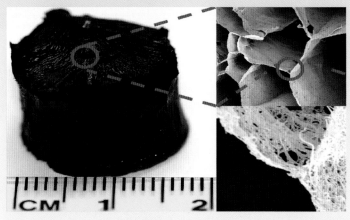

free movement of ideas between virtual and physical realms, unfettered by the manufacturing constraints and transportation limitations of prior industrial era approaches. The structural frame has since begun to morph into a hybrid skeleton/surface in which materials are employed more efficiently and purposefully—deposited in layered strata reminiscent of the original earthen architecture.

Material Basis and Behaviors

To comprehensively understand our geosphere, we must engage it at multiple scales, from mineralogy (the study of minerals and their properties) to seismology (the study of earthquakes, seismic waves, and tectonic plate movement). It is a sphere so encompassing that it touches, in one way or another, every other natural sphere on the planet.

The most basic building blocks of the geosphere, found in all rocks except obsidian, coal, and amber, are minerals. Four criteria must be met in order for something to be called a mineral. First, it must be inorganic (not formed from plants or animals). Second, it must be naturally occurring (not made by humans). Third, it must have the same chemical composition no matter where it is found. Fourth, it must have a crystalline structure (its atoms line up in a particular repeating geometry). Fig. 3

Minerals fall into one of two categories, metallic and nonmetallic. Most elements on the periodic table are metallics. Metallics are relatively easy to identify: they conduct both heat and electricity, they are

malleable, they are ductile, they possess a shiny luster, they are opaque as a thin sheet, and they are solid at room temperature. The vast differences between metals and nonmetals have traditionally made certain minerals attractive for particular architectural uses.

When we think of the geosphere, most people first think of rocks. Rocks are composed of one or several minerals. Geologists test for specific characteristics in order to classify minerals: color, shape, hardness (based on the Mohs Hardness Scale), streak (the color of powder left over when a mineral is scratched on a ceramic surface), and luster (the way light reflects off the mineral). Rocks might contain any combination of thousands of minerals; however, only ten are found in a majority of the rocks found in the earth's crust: plagioclase, quartz, orthoclase, amphibole, pyroxene, olivine, calcite, biotite, garnet, and clay.[8]

Rocks are categorized by how they are formed. Igneous rocks are formed from cooling magma, sedimentary rocks are generally the result of eroded rock particles settling in layers that are compressed under pressure, and when even more pressure is exerted and extreme heat is added, metamorphic rocks are formed.

How rocks move through these different stages—transporting and transforming themselves over time—is called the *rock cycle*. Just as there is a hydrologic cycle accounting for all water movement on the planet, there is a similar, but much slower, rock cycle. In this cycle, metamorphic rock is broken down to form either sedimentary or igneous rock. The same is true in the other directions of this relationship. The movement of the earth's plates, caused by convection currents in the planet's mantle, is responsible for progressing the rock cycle. Rocks are continuously pulled down into the earth's core and pushed up onto its surface.

While we may not observe this relatively slow process, it is remarkably dynamic and powerful. The designers in this chapter embrace the long duration of geological formation, either in the way they conceive of constructing their work or in the materials they choose. The work questions the limited ways in which we approach building construction, think about building life cycle, and predetermine the outcome of our creative work.

Technology

Humanity's increasingly sophisticated interactions with the geosphere led to the rise of civilization. Agriculture, metallurgy, architecture, and cities relied on the land and its extractable resources. Reinforcing the significance of this connection, historians designated the important early phases of civilization— the Stone Age, the Bronze Age, and the Iron Age— based on notable earth-based material technologies. The development of tools and decorative objects during these periods involved a variety of approaches ranging from simple harvesting and refinement (sharpening of stone implements) to the emulation of powerful geologic processes (melting of metals from ore). Throughout history, the frontier of material technology has largely been defined by the attainment of unprecedented performance. The identification and cultivation of desirable characteristics, such as strength, durability, and lightness, exemplify the pursuit of the hypernatural: superior material properties coaxed out of existing resources. In the geosphere this quest has increasingly focused on the microscopic structures of materials, as well as the imaginative combinations of different materials.

Today, no material represents the search for super-strength like carbon. One of the first known elements and the fourth-most abundant element in the universe, carbon has a variety of allotropes that range considerably in their physical characteristics. Russian scientists Konstantin Novoselov and Andre Geim's discovery of graphene—the strongest and thinnest material known at the that time they received

the Nobel Prize in 2010—added another high-performance allotrope to a list including tubular (carbon nanotube) and spherical ("buckyball") forms.[9] In 2013 Rice University researchers discovered carbyne, a carbon allotrope twice as strong as graphene, with a simpler atomic form than that of other allotropes. According to theoretical physicist Boris Yakobson, carbyne represents "the strongest possible assembly of atoms" and is being developed for new sensors, nanomechanical systems, and energy storage devices.[10] Carbon has also been used to create some of the lightest known materials, such as aerographite and multiwalled carbon nanotube (MWCNT) aerogel, which boast low densities of 200 mg/cm^3 and 4 mg/cm^3, respectively.[11] Fig. 4 In addition, carbon scientists have employed other common elements in the search for threshold-breaking performance. The world's lightest material, for example, is composed of a nickel phosphorous microstructured lattice, with a density of only 0.9 mg/cm^3.[12] Another ultrastrong material is made of silica nanofibers and is fifteen times stronger than steel and ten times stronger than glass-reinforced plastic (GRP).[13] Researchers have also developed materials with adjustable characteristics, such as a metal that transforms between a strong and inflexible state to a soft and pliable state, and a new form of silicone that increases in strength while under compression.[14]

Experimentation with geological materials has resulted in novel combinations of physical properties. For example, an emerging category of materials called amorphous metals combines desirable characteristics of metal and glass. So-called *glassy metals* exhibit an unprecedented combination of strength and toughness, without the brittleness of glass or the deformability of metal. Amorphous metals may also be highly conductive like metal and transparent like glass, such as palladium alloy glass created by the Lawrence Berkeley National Laboratory, which exhibits the best-known combination of strength and toughness of any material.[15] The emphasis on transparency and conductivity has been especially important for the development of renewable energy technologies, such as solar-harvesting window films made with transparent hexagonal fullerene carbon or silver nanowires.[16] Unlike conventional photovoltaic panels, these technologies allow uninterrupted visibility in glazed

5. Ceramic paper, by the
University of Stuttgart and
the Max Planck Institute.

facades. Other notable mineral mash-ups include
stanene, which is made from arranging tin atoms like
graphene and is the only known material with 100
percent conduction efficiency; vanadium pentoxide
ceramic, a ceramic paper that combines the durability
of ceramics and the flexibility of paper; and nanoparticle polymer materials that combine the conductivity
of metal and the ductility of plastic.[17] Fig. 5

Despite groundbreaking achievements like these,
the world of geosphere-based materials confronts
serious environmental challenges. Mineral extraction
and processing are occurring at ever-increasing rates,
and today humanity obtains most of its resources
from nonrenewable materials. Our dependency on
nonrenewables—whether they are common materials
like oil or uncommon ones like rare earth metals—
increases the likelihood of geopolitical conflicts
and international market volatility. The typical U.S.
citizen consumes over ten tons of materials annually,
and the global average is growing twice as fast.[18]
The increasing global consumption of mineral
resources points to an ever-more turbulent economic
and environmental future, particularly since most
virgin nonrenewable materials require significant
amounts of embodied energy and carbon dioxide.
However, many of these materials may be recycled
or converted to fuel at much lower environmental
costs—making the case for an effective, closed-loop
cycle for existing technical nutrients. Fulfillment of
this goal will require the development of more efficient and versatile recycling technologies, improved
recycling infrastructure, and more effective environmental policies.

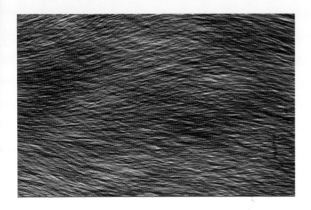

Application

Of all the natural science domains, architecture has
the most intimate connection with the geosphere.
The oldest records of human habitation are contained
within the mineral surface of the earth—in places like
the rocky outcrops of the Ethiopian Kibish Mountains
(195,000 BCE) or Klasies River Caves in South Africa
(125,000 BCE).[19] Based on their durability, earthen
materials often persevere for millennia, making them
appropriate not only as the substance of shelter but
also as a lasting record of human existence. This
abiding quality had significance on the histories of
architecture and landscape architecture. In concrete
terms human constructions carve into the landscape
(subtraction), spring from the earth (addition), or are
built with raw materials from the land (utilization).
Symbolically, earth and stone are employed to represent other materials or contexts—such as the acanthus
leaf capitals of Corinthian columns or the portrayal
of the universe in Japanese *karesansui* rock gardens.
This multifaceted approach continues today, but with
an emphasis on the performance of geospheric materials and the processes that shape them.

Digital fabrication has transformed the architectural application of mineral-based materials in
profound ways, including the fabrication of novel
substances made from mineral resources. Many
earth-derived materials may now be utilized in both
additive and subtractive manufacturing, including
relatively novel variants like concrete and stone.
Increasingly, mineral applications may be digitally
fabricated on-site as well as in controlled environments. For example, University of Southern California
engineers are developing a site-based concrete printing method called Contour Crafting, which is capable
of producing a 2,500-square-foot (232 sq. m) house
in twenty hours.[20] Architects like Janjaap Ruijssenaars
and Shiro Studio have been experimenting with the
D-Shape printer—devised by London-based engineer
Enrico Dini—to print some of the first building structures in synthetic marble.[21] Dini himself has employed
the technology to print artificial reefs from seabed
sludge to support marine habitats. Stone Spray is
another notable on-site mineral-printing technology.
Created by architects Anna Kulik, Petr Novikov, and
Inder Shergill, it uses a mechanical armature to spray
a mixture of earth and a solidifying agent to form

compression-based structures.[22] Unlike other printing technologies, Stone Spray is not limited to bottom-up layered constructions, but can generate objects in nearly any direction. Other compelling approaches include Brian Peters's 3-D printed ceramic bricks and Markus Kayser's Solar Sinter, a sunlight-powered 3-D printer that transforms desert sand into glass structures.[23]

Architects and engineers have also been advancing the capabilities of earth-based materials, with the goal to create a more resilient built environment. Researchers at Michigan Technological University developed a method to reinforce roadbeds with nanoclay—nanoparticles of layered mineral silicates that can be combined with polymers and other substances to make high-performance nanocomposites.[24] Scientists at the University of Illinois, Delft University of Technology, Yonsei University, and other institutions have developed varieties of self-healing concrete based on the formation of calcium carbonate or calcium hydroxide, cement matrix swelling, or the release of microencapsulated polymer healing agents. The University of Michigan's Engineered Cement Composite is currently used to patch cracked concrete in highway construction as well as provide enhanced shear resistance in high-rise buildings.[25] In both cases, the concrete adds significant resilience, since the material is five hundred times more crack-resistant than regular concrete. It can also incorporate sensing and self-repair capabilities, making it function similarly to human skin. In this way, earthen materials are becoming more

lifelike, indicating a blurring between the geosphere and biosphere.

The experiential richness of the geosphere has inspired architects to mimic its physiognomy. Antoine Predock's McNamara Alumni Center geode in Minneapolis (2000), Peter Eisenman's quarry-like Memorial to the Murdered Jews of Europe in Berlin (2005), and Zaha Hadid's slot canyon–inspired Galaxy Soho in Beijing (2012) all convey the visual potency of the abiding geological landscape. Figs. 6 and 7 Aranda\Lasch's *Modern Primitives* installations at the 2010 Venice Architecture Biennale explore the geometry of microcrystalline mineral structures at an enlarged scale.[26] This type of geomimicry is not limited to aesthetic concerns, but includes functional considerations. Engineers at Penn State University, for example, are investigating the connections between responsive geometries and performance in an effort called "predictive multi-scale modeling," which aims to advance the morphological capacities of smart materials for a variety of applications.[27]

Bricktopia

Barcelona, Spain, 2013
MAP13

The architectural vault is a form of the constructed cave. Like the natural subterranean void spaces that humans have used for shelter since prehistoric times, vaulting allows for the creation of mineral-based, structural ceilings that provide cover from the elements. The Catalan vault is a form of vault construction that minimizes thrust. Also called *bóveda tabicada* or the timbrel vault, the Catalan was originally developed in Mesopotamia and later spread throughout Europe during the Middle Ages.[28] Unlike gravity-reliant vaults composed of bricks arranged on their sides, the Catalan vault consists of several thin layers of bricks or tiles laid flat in an overlapping pattern, set with quick-drying mortar. Popularized by architects like Antoni Gaudí and Rafael Guastavino, the Catalan vault is a form of lightweight, thin-shell construction that can assume a shallower, more graceful profile than Roman vaults.

Although load-bearing masonry construction declined with the advent of the modern frame, brick-based vaulted structures are making a comeback—thanks to the assistance of new digital tools. Architectural engineer Philippe Block's rhinoVAULT plug-in software developed at the ETH Zurich facilitates the virtual simulation of complex Catalan vaults made from multiple layers of thin bricks.[29] One of the best examples of the application of this software is Bricktopia, a structure designed by MAP13 architects for the 2013 International Festival of Architecture (Eme3) in Barcelona. Situated in an enclosed forecourt of a nineteenth-century brick-clad factory, Bricktopia was conceived as a multifunctional pavilion for festival activities. MAP13 created a variety of spatial experiences within single undulating shell structure, including voids of varying scale, accessible openings, and a large roof oculus. In this way, the pavilion demonstrates the complete integration and blurring of conventionally disparate architectural elements—wall, column, roof, room, door, window, and skylight are all seamlessly assembled by the sophisticated deployment of one monolithic structural skin.

Bricktopia represents not only the reinvigoration of masonry construction but also the drive to realize new compression-only structures of unprecedented complexity and versatility. Bricktopia is simultaneously contemporary and ancient: on the one hand, it exhibits computationally assisted capabilities in thin-shell vaulted construction, while on the other, it resembles a heterogeneous collection of geomorphic void structures found in naturally formed caverns.

GEOtube Tower

Dubai, United Arab Emirates, 2009
Faulders Studio

A number of recent geologically driven projects leverage natural materials and processes to contribute to the fabrication, assembly, construction, and operations of their buildings. This is sometimes referred to as *geoengineering*. GEOtube Tower in Dubai by Faulders Studio is "a new kind of urban sculptural icon." Once constructed, this building is hardly "finished." Instead, a geologic skin is grown on its outer surface through natural salt deposition.

To facilitate this deposition, concentrated salt water is delivered to the GEOtube Tower via a 2.87-mile (4.62 km) buried pipeline, connecting the building to the Persian Gulf, which has the world's highest oceanic water salinity. Upon arrival at the building, the water is carried up its facade through a series of organically arrayed vascular pipes and then misted onto the tower's transparent skin. As the water evaporates in the sun, a thin coat of white salt is left behind, gradually transforming the building from transparent to translucent to opaque. Over time, the spatial territory of the tower's facade transforms into a natural habitat supporting local wildlife and an accessible surface for harvesting crystal salt, a process that is estimated to take over fifteen years.

The visual, spatial, and luminous character of the building migrates along with these changes in ways that are unpredictably dependent on the deposition behavior. This behavior is of course contingent on issues like orientation, wind speed, humidity levels, and temperature. The architectural character of the building will vary, not along a linear trajectory, but in the rising and falling waves of shifts from season to season and year to year.

What may be GEOtube Tower's most lucid contribution to contemporary discourse around fabrication and construction is the notion that a building can be minimally scaffolded with imported materials early in its life cycle, then completed later through an automated process of locally harvested materials. That a building's structural system might also provide the very means for its skin's self-assembly is appropriate and ethical in a world economy where materials are prohibitively expensive to transport and labor is increasingly costly.

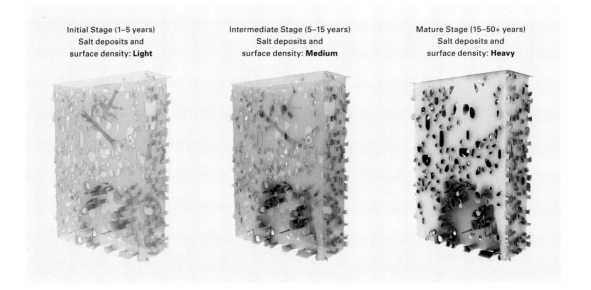

Initial Stage (1–5 years)
Salt deposits and
surface density: **Light**

Intermediate Stage (5–15 years)
Salt deposits and
surface density: **Medium**

Mature Stage (15–50+ years)
Salt deposits and
surface density: **Heavy**

Lithuanian Pavilion

Yeosu, South Korea, 2012
Mečislovas and Martynas Valevičius

Amber is a biological product transformed into a geological material. The resin from a tree that has been fossilized over time, amber has been prized since prehistoric times for its translucent golden luster. Amber is also appreciated for its preservation of the earth's ecological record. Since amber specimens often contain plant matter or insects that became trapped in the sticky resin, the material acts as a window into early life. Amber samples have been found with animal inclusions up to 230 million years old.

Amber forms in a two-stage process. First, tree resin is converted via high temperature and pressure into copal, a polymer with a gummy texture. The material eventually loses its terpenes—or aromatic hydrocarbons—resulting in its final, solid form. One of the most valued types of fossilized resin is Baltic amber, which comes from the Sciadopityaceae plants that grew in what was once a subtropical forest in northern Europe.[30] Now found scattered on the shores of the Baltic Sea, amber is the national gemstone of Lithuania, where it is an abundant resource and the subject of popular folktales.

For their design of the Lithuanian pavilion at the Yeosu Expo in 2012, architects Mečislovas and Martynas Valevičius created a space with a singular focus on amber. Visitors to the pavilion received the immediate impression of being immersed in an amber-infused container, reminiscent of the Eocene-era buried riverbeds that contain rich deposits of the resin. The designers created a simple interior room wrapped in amber-colored surfaces, including an underlit, gold-colored floor with a pearlescent sheen. A series of bollard-style vitrines displayed fine specimens of amber under illuminated magnifying lenses, revealing trapped ferns, spiders, and a lizard from the primordial Baltic forests. With this purposeful focus, the Lithuanian pavilion is both a paleontological museum and an immersive geomimetic environment—a multifaceted setting that successfully conveys the story of this country's natural riches.

London, England, 2009
Shiro Studio

Radiolaria, a project by Shiro Studio, learns from the slow system of deposition found in the geological process of sedimentary rock formation. It was developed in partnership with the additive manufacturing company D-Shape. Similar to the process of sedimentary rock formation, additive manufacturing—or 3-D printing—is a technology used to make prototypes through successively layering materials such as cornstarch, plastic, and metal. Increasingly, however, additive manufacturing is used to produce final products themselves. While this makes sense for small artifacts like jewelry, buildings pose a much greater challenge because of their size, complexity, and need for structural reliability.

Radiolaria is one of the first successful uses of architectural-scale printing with natural rock dust. It is a 953-cubic-foot (27 cu. m) freestanding pavilion made from an artificial sandstone material held together with an inorganic binder. With remarkable strength characteristics, this binder allows the pavilion to span a relatively large distance without the need for steel reinforcement. It effectively transforms marble dust, sand, or rock particles into a solid mineral with microcrystalline characteristics that are chemically neutral and easily recyclable. Radiolaria is higher in resolution than previous experiments with full-scale additive manufacturing, and, like natural sedimentary rock formations, its complexity grows without the use of provisional, temporary formwork or disposable, expensive molds. Further, the project eliminates carbon-emitting portland cement, waste material, contractor error, and contractor injuries. It can be fabricated from either imported or native material.

By modeling a natural process as opposed to a natural form, Radiolaria contributes in a broad and significant way to geoarchitectural research. How it learns from observations about natural manufacturing processes is significant. Its advancements offer new manufacturing solutions to a building industry plagued by outdated, stagnant, and often poisonous construction technologies.

▼ 3-D printing process, showing deposition of liquid binder

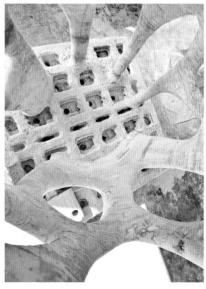

▲ Interior view showing structure base

Seizure

Yorkshire, England, 2008
Roger Hiorns

Mineral hydration is a process in which water interacts with a mineral's crystalline structure. This chemical reaction often occurs during metasomatism, a transformation of igneous or metamorphic rock by hydrothermal fluids. Mineral hydration can either destroy or create: it is a common weathering process that accelerates mineral decomposition, but is also a way to develop new crystalline lattice structures. A mineral that readily forms such structures via hydration is copper sulfate ($CuSO_4$), which is visible as a bright blue crystalline layer known as chalcanthite (or copper flower) in oxidizing copper deposits.[31]

London-based artist Roger Hiorns became captivated by copper sulfate's ability to precipitate within a chemical solution, because for him it represented nature determining its own aesthetic outcomes. He experimented with the material in works such as *Copper Sulphate Chartres & Copper Sulphate Notre-Dame* (1996) and *Before the Rain* (2003), in both cases growing a new skin of blue crystals on models of Gothic structures. Inspired by the architectural implications of the process, Hiorns set out to create a full-scale, inhabitable environment.

In 2008 the artist secured an empty apartment in Southwark, London, and ordered two shipping containers of copper sulfate. After sealing the exterior of the flat, he filled the entire space with the blue powder and seventy-five thousand liters of water. Hiorns allowed the mineral bath to sit for about a month, checking it daily for signs of positive growth. Draining the solution revealed a glimmering blue space encrusted with layers of triclinic crystals of copper sulfate pentahydrate ($CuSO_4 \cdot 5H_2O$)—the physical outgrowth of the hydration reaction. Reminiscent of an ice cave mixed with an Yves Klein blue painting, *Seizure* is the result of a natural process applied at an immersive scale in uncontaminated form—as opposed to the relatively small, variegated manifestation commonly seen in nature. Unfortunately, *Seizure* will not retain its electric blue color in perpetuity, as a reverse process will eventually transform the crystals back to copper sulfate—a fitting end for an environment constructed by nature.

ATMOSPHERE

ATMOSPHERE

In "A Home Is Not a House," architectural critic Reyner Banham writes, "When your house contains such a complex of piping, flues, ducts, wires, lights, inlets, outlets, ovens, sinks, refuse disposers, hi-fi reverberators, antennae, conduits, freezers, heaters—when it contains so many services that the hardware could stand up by itself without any assistance from the house, why have the house to hold it up?"[1] The elegant Stratus Project by RVTR directly confronts Banham's provocation. While appearing as a simple, static surface, the project is actually a "kinetic, sensing and environment-responsive interior envelope system."[2] It is a material assembly that conflates the functions of envelope and building mechanics into a single system, ostensibly "holding up" the house with an enveloping technological network.

The first physical prototype of the Stratus Project is a dynamic suspended ceiling composed of a thin cable–tensegrity structure married to a thick array of translucent cells. Occupants, which RVTR refers to as *breathers*, affect the atmospheric conditions under the ceiling by simply traversing under it at different speeds or by lingering under it for various lengths of time (see pp 50–51). The system senses locations and quantities of breathers through an array of distributed sensors. It then reacts by automatically providing illumination and altering spatial climatic conditions. *Breathing cells*, which form the visible surface of the system, are actuated to open and close like fish gills in order to extract air from or infuse air into a micro-environment below. The system senses conditions like movement, temperature, and the presence of carbon dioxide and air pollutants before triggering the intelligent surface's actuators, lights, and microfans to produce invisible pockets of intimate atmospheres. These subtly demarcated spatial boundaries form rooms of mutable size and shape without the need for conventional walls.

The Stratus Project is atmospheric on multiple levels. First, its thick surface textile embodies the layering, depth, shadowing, and translucence of a dense fog. It is constantly morphing into new patterns, porosities, and shapes like a cloud floating across the sky. More significant, however, is its ability to produce literal atmospheres. As a breathing architectural surface, it can render adjacent spaces simultaneously cool and warm, light and dark, and moist and dry.

Herein lies the hallmark of all work contributing to this chapter on atmosphere: the capacity to produce an architecture of invisibility, or to delineate space without reliance on physical material.

Background

The history of humanity's relationship with the atmosphere is a remarkable account of our transformation from a tractable, deity-fearing species to an enlightened and empowered population. Although we once cowered in ignorance and supplication before the storm, today we understand many of the physical and chemical causes of atmospheric phenomena, and exert a measurable influence over the climate through processes such as cloud seeding and climate-modifying carbon emissions. The story of Prometheus is symbolic of this transition: when the mythological champion of men stole fire from Zeus, he effectively bequeathed a heavenly tool to his mortal friends, thus enabling them with godlike powers. Fig. 1 This fable has come to be associated with both the increasing potency and hubris of humanity, heralding the wonders of technological development while admonishing the perils of striving beyond acceptable boundaries. Just as Prometheus received a grim punishment for his misdeed, we now face an ominous future shaped by the unintended consequences of our exploitation of fire. Specifically, by harnessing this Olympian gift to its fullest potential, we unleashed the flame of modern industry—with disastrous climatological effects. Today, we seek to employ a variety of strategies to recalibrate the atmosphere to its previous, less-volatile state.

Climate directly influenced the development of early civilization, which flourished in the warm regions of Mesopotamia, the Indus Valley, and the Nile. The inhabitants of the first city-states benefited from environmental conditions that supported the development of agriculture, such as adequate sunlight and rainfall, but were susceptible to the negative effects of unpredictable weather patterns. Recent studies point to climate change as a more potent influence of historic events than previously thought—with one investigation blaming an immense drought that occurred about 3,200 years ago for the collapse of Late Bronze Age Mediterranean societies.[3] The potentially disastrous consequences of unpredictable

weather events motivated early humans to exert control over their domains, resulting in the development of more effective resource-harvesting and preservation technologies (e.g., irrigation and grain storage) as well as more robust forms of shelter. Arguably, the first concept of sustainability would not have been the preservation of natural cycles but the establishment of human control over them. Architecture itself was born out of the desire to control one's atmospheric surroundings in the form of shelter from the elements. Our contemporary urbanized planet owes its existence to the effective instrument of building, which has enabled human societies to thrive—especially in parts of the globe previously considered uninhabitable.

If architecture indeed originated out of the aspiration to control climate, then modernism represents the apotheosis of this desire. While preindustrial construction methods—from masonry walls to shoji screens—offered loose, imperfect means of environmental regulation, modern building technologies aimed for total control. Fig. 2 For centuries, heating methods such as the hearth, furnace, or hydronic piping were fundamental for human survival in cold climates. However, the invention of air conditioning—especially when combined with heating and ventilation—enabled absolute climate management. Banham

claims that "by providing almost total control of the atmospheric variables of temperature, humidity, and purity, [air conditioning] has demolished almost all of the environmental constraints on design...For anyone who is prepared to foot the consequent bill for power consumed, it is now possible to live in almost any time or form of house one likes to name in any region of the world that takes the fancy."[4] Yet for its extraordinary benefits, air conditioning has its own Promethean consequences; it is now known to be a leading cause of global warming and ozone depletion.[5] Today architects and engineers are engaged in a hybrid approach to indoor climate management: reducing energy use and reconnecting hermetically sheltered building occupants with the outdoors while maintaining an optimal level of control.

Material Basis and Behaviors
Our built structures keep us warm and dry as they defend us from fluctuations in humidity, wind, temperature, and precipitation. Modern building envelopes effectively separate one atmosphere (outside) from another (inside). However, in the earth's atmosphere, sharp boundaries form without any material delineation, at the confluence of dissimilar air pressures, temperatures, and humidities. The

Stratus Project

RVTR refers to occupants of the stratus project as "breathers." The Stratus Project is designed to register the presence of the "breather" in a variety of ways and use that information to trigger designed responses.

"BREATHERS"

Environmental Responses
The physical presence of each individual is detected in a variety of ways. "Breathers" generate heat, carbon dioxide, movement, and pollutants. They also make noise. Distributed sensors register these atmospheric triggers and use the input to actuate a series of distributed elements that modify the environment.

1. Carbon Dioxide

2. Temperature

3. Motion

INPUT FROM OUTPUT

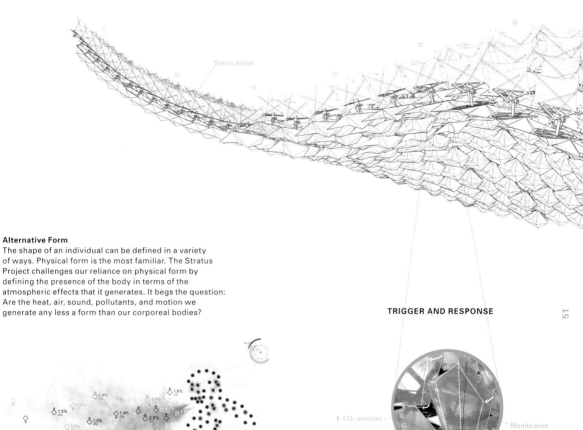

Servo motor

Alternative Form

The shape of an individual can be defined in a variety of ways. Physical form is the most familiar. The Stratus Project challenges our reliance on physical form by defining the presence of the body in terms of the atmospheric effects that it generates. It begs the question: Are the heat, air, sound, pollutants, and motion we generate any less a form than our corporeal bodies?

TRIGGER AND RESPONSE

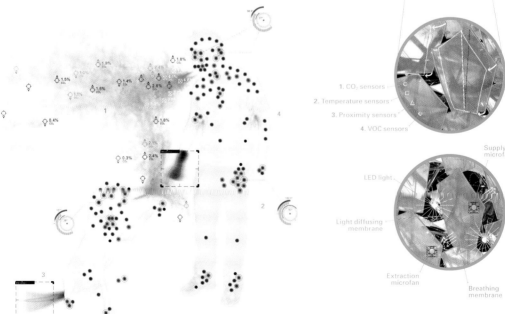

1. CO_2 sensors
2. Temperature sensors
3. Proximity sensors
4. VOC sensors

Membranes actuate in response to input from "breathers"

Supply air microfan

LED light

Light diffusing membrane

Extraction microfan

Breathing membrane

AN ETHEREAL PRESENCE

Atmosphere

3. The earth's atmosphere
viewed at sunset from
space shuttle Atlantis, 2010

meteorological term for this confluence is a front.[6] We feel fronts as they move through a region; the air gets colder, it feels drier, or the sky grows cloudy. Manuel De Landa says that our world is composed of various pressures, small and large, all struggling for control in a constant search for equilibrium. In our atmosphere these pressure differentials result in powerful weather patterns, which, De Landa asserts, are like giant, self-assembled motors:

A hurricane is a motor in the literal sense, a motor defined as something with a heat reservoir that circulates heat through a Carnot cycle via differences of temperature. When a hurricane is born, a lot of self-organizing processes are involved that bring heat from the outside and concentrate it into a reservoir. In other words, it's a self-assembled motor.[7]

We can take motors to mean sources of energy in this context. Architects researching atmospheric energy (differences in temperature, pressure, and humidity) can produce spatial boundaries as effectively as they can with brick, concrete, or wood. To understand how, it is important to understand the term *atmosphere* along with the conditions contributing to its potent energy.

The atmosphere is a collection of gases that make earth inhabitable. It is composed of 78 percent nitrogen, 21 percent oxygen, 1 percent water vapor, and trace amounts of other gases like carbon dioxide and argon. The atmosphere absorbs ultraviolet radiation from the sun to warm the planet. It is composed of five different zones, decreasing in density from inner to outer: the troposphere, 0 to 6 miles (0–10 km) above earth's surface; the stratosphere, 6 to 31 miles (10–50 km); the mesosphere, 31 to 53 miles (50–85 km); the thermosphere, 53 to 217 miles (85–350 km); and finally, the exosphere, where particles are so far apart that they can travel hundreds of miles without colliding with one another. Fig. 3

Several factors affect atmospheric conditions on earth. The first is temperature. During the day, the atmosphere is warmed by the sun; at night, when the sun sets, it cools. Temperature differentials are a primary cause of many weather conditions, like thunderstorms. The second property is pressure, which is a measure of air density. When two adjacent regions have different pressures, swirling winds result as an attempt to restore balance. The third property is humidity, which is a measure of water vapor in the air. The humidity level is indicative of conditions like precipitation, dew, and fog. Temperature, air pressure, and humidity all work in concert with one another in complex ways. For example, humidity is a *selective absorber* of heat.[8] This means that it allows green light to pass through, but it absorbs red light, like infrared energy radiated from the earth's surface. For this reason, humid, hot regions trap warm air and remain hot in the evening, while arid, hot regions, like deserts, lose their heat at night and experience significant temperature drops.

Atmospheric conditions are complex and difficult to control. But when managed carefully, building-scale microclimates and atmospheric phenomena

can produce subtle and nuanced spatial qualities that
are nearly impossible with conventional building
materials.

Technology

In the twentieth century the building industry aimed
to create the perfect indoor environment—one in
which temperature, humidity, and lighting could all
be set at optimal levels, regardless of external
conditions. Although architects frequently sought
to reduce visual barriers between the interior and
exterior, the physical separation between the two
realms increased with the steadfast goal to devise a
comprehensively engineered interior climate. Fixed
glazing increasingly replaced operable windows, and
the widespread use of air conditioning and availability
of cheap energy made external demands on building
envelopes irrelevant. Surprisingly, the 1970s oil crisis
only exacerbated the situation, for despite the energy
conservation measures it prompted, it also led to
introverted buildings—with larger floor plates, darker
glazing, lower ceilings, and flat fluorescent lighting.
However, after decades of "sick building" syndrome
and a general disaffection with characterless, hermetic
interiors, architecture has begun to rediscover the
great outdoors.

Lighting is now a fundamental concern of indoor
environmental quality, and studies have proved
strong connections between the natural daylight
spectrum and the well-being of building occupants.[9]
Daylighting is now a major component of lighting
design, and architects seek to provide adequate

sunlight while minimizing energy consumption—
a difficult task given the inherent conflicts between
glazing and thermal control. There is now a wide
assortment of exterior and interior shading devices
designed to minimize this incongruity, with some
of the most advanced products offering integral
shading. Glazing coatings are also a promising territory of research: for example, Fraunhofer Institute
scientists devised a new blue-selective coating for
windows after determining that human biorhythms
are more sensitive to blue light than other parts of
the spectrum.[10] Remote daylighting technologies,
such as fiber optic– or mirror-based ducts, serve
sunlight-deprived spaces in buildings based on the
light propagation principles of total internal reflection
(TIR). Scientists have also been able to enhance the
color rendering index (CRI) of artificial light sources,
and technologies such as tunable white LEDs and
field-induced polymer electroluminescence (FIPEL)
offer better simulations of sunlight than conventional
approaches.[11]

Air handling systems have also become more
sophisticated, and mechanical engineers now rou-
tinely collaborate with architects on the performance
design of operable facades—a significant change
from past, internally focused practices. Increased
access to outside air has encouraged more advanced
approaches to managing airflow, and techniques like
underfloor air delivery, displacement ventilation, and
multiple-skin facades privilege air movement over
traditional air conditioning for cooling. Refrigeration
is also becoming more effective, with systems such
as Freeaire—a technology that delivers outdoor air
to coolers and freezers when the exterior temperature
is sufficiently cold.[12] Designers are also exploring
air as a medium of expression and have developed
tunable vapor-based technologies, such as FogScreen,
a thin curtain of mist that operates as a translucent
projection display, or Micasa LAB's Nebula 12, a
liquid nitrogen and hot water–infused pendant that
generates its own cloud.[13] Fig. 4

The architectural engagement of air now extends
beyond the building envelope. SMIT's hybrid cladding
systems Grow and Solar Ivy, for example, employ
both flexible organic photovoltaic films and piezoelectric generators to harness energy.[14] When the PV
modules are moved by the wind, the kinetic motion

5. Cloud seeding
equipment installed on
a Cessna 210 plane

6. Teshima Art Museum, by
Ryue Nishizawa and Rei Naito,
Teshima, Japan, 2010

is converted into usable power. A similar technology is Vibro-Wind, a Cornell University–based invention that utilizes wind-induced oscillation to produce energy, as opposed to the air-slicing action of traditional turbines.[15] Scientists have accelerated the development of wind-harnessing technologies and strategies for climate modification. Cloud seeding, for example, employs a variety of methods to change the weather by inducing or suppressing precipitation.[16] Fig. 5 Materials like silver iodide, liquid propane, dry ice, and salt are commonly used to encourage the formation of ice crystals to produce rain or snow. Cloud seeding is now actively used by dozens of nations to mitigate drought, reduce the formation of hailstones, and prevent fog formation at airports.[17] Once considered a fantasy, the practice of weather modification represents an unprecedented human capacity: designing the architecture of the atmosphere itself.

Application

In architecture, the term *atmosphere* is used to describe the immaterial qualities of space. Although dictionaries associate a different meaning with interior atmosphere than with the air and sky, it is actually the same concept applied at different scales—reinforcing the idea of architectural space as a microcosm or fragment of the firmament. According to architect Peter Zumthor, "We perceive atmosphere

through our emotional sensibility—a form of perception that works incredibly quickly, and which we humans evidently need to help us survive."[18] This immediate, visceral response to one's surroundings is a self-preservation mechanism, the origins of which predate architecture and influenced the establishment of early sacred sites within the primeval landscape. In the Japanese Shinto religion, for example, the term *kehai* meant the "atmospheric indication of sacredness that the lay of the land itself might express."[19] Today, architectural atmosphere can be used to describe any kind of ambience—however, it also refers to a growing number of works that make stronger connections to the actual atmosphere.

At a conceptual level, atmosphere is invoked when describing the deliberate emptiness created in spaces of minimal physical features. Architects of the Japanese White School, for example, design elemental, abstract works in which materials are employed to impart a sense of immateriality.[20] This approach is epitomized in Ryue Nishizawa's Teshima Art Museum, a project that uses minimal means to maximum sensory effect. Fig. 6 Composed of a single thin-shelled concrete pod structure with no columns, Nishizawa's collaboration with sculptor Rei Naito houses just one work of art: a piece called *Matrix* that consists of groundwater seeping up through the floor. Elliptical, razor-edged oculi provide dramatic views of the sky within the upper surface, while the lower surface exhibits continually shifting pools of water that reflect this view. The result is a focused experience situated within the thickened threshold between land and sky—architecture at its most minimal and primeval state.

Other designers have combined conceptual notions of atmosphere with the literal sensation of floating. For example, Tomás Saraceno's 2013 *In Orbit* installation in the K21 Ständehaus of the Kunstsammlung Nordrhein-Westfalen invited viewers to become suspended more than eighty feet (25 m) above ground. The project consisted of multiple levels of giant steel cable nets held apart by six large transparent or reflective PVC balls with strategically placed voids allowing movement from one level to another. Because of the steel cables' and spheres' near-visual immateriality, the occupants of the work appeared to hover miraculously—like the bowler hat–clad men in René Magritte's *Golconda*. Numen/For Use designed a similarly uplifting installation called *Net Blow-Up* on the Yokohama waterfront. Composed of a large, inflated container with multiple levels of interwoven black mesh, the project imparted a similar physical experience—yet a vastly different visual effect—from *In Orbit*. Whereas Saraceno's installation downplayed its own physical presence, *Net Blow-Up* dematerialized the container itself with the use of translucent, backlit fabric—creating the effect of inhabitants and meshed surfaces floating within a void.

Net Blow-Up is one example in a vibrant history of inflatable structures. From the eighteenth-century invention of the hot-air balloon to Diller Scofidio + Renfro's proposed Expansion Bubble for the Hirshhorn Museum in Washington, D.C., the impetus to create an architecture of air has resulted in the enclosure of large volumes with minimal substance. Installed in 2013 artist Christo's *Big Air Package* was the largest freestanding inflated envelope in existence. Located within a former gas container in Germany, *Big Air Package* possessed a volume of over six million cubic feet (177,000 cu. m) and was nearly 300 feet (90 m) tall and over 160 feet (50 m) in diameter. Christo likened the enclosure of semitransparent polyester fabric—which maintained inflation at 27 pascals of constant pressure by two fans—to a 300-foot-high (90 m) cathedral.[21]

If inflatable structures are largely composed of air, other designs attempt to harness it. Environmental artist Ned Kahn is known for his wind-activated facades, in addition to other works that incorporate natural forces. His expansive 2010 installation at Target Field in Minneapolis—known as *The Wave*—employs tens of thousands of hinged aluminum tiles suspended on cables. Fig. 7 As wind gusts interact with the six-hundred-by-sixty-foot (180 by 18 m) vertical field, the tiles make apparent the dynamic and complex patterns of airflow, which are otherwise visually imperceptible. Other notable wind-channeling works include James Murray and Shota Vashakmadze's proposed Scene Sensor, an open-air pavilion for New York's Freshkills Park that harnesses wind with a piezoelectric wire-mesh facade; Najla El Zein's London *Wind Portal* installation made of five thousand vertically suspended windmills, and Delatchew Arkitekter's Strawscraper, a proposed conversion of a Stockholm high-rise into a cilia-covered vertical wind farm. Like the conceptual approaches previously described, these projects, and the case studies that follow, demonstrate an elevated connection between the atmosphere of architecture and the atmosphere of the firmament—and create a bridge between the invisible and the visible.

The Cloud

Shanghai, China, 2013
Schmidt Hammer Lassen Architects

"The Cloud pavilion is the quintessence of lightness, immateriality, and fuzziness."[22] Designed as a temporary pavilion for the Shanghai West Bund Biennial for Architecture and Contemporary Art, the project is noteworthy for its ability to produce an atmospheric effect through a very common, everyday material: white rope. Thousands of rope strands that are cut to varying lengths hang from the ceiling of an otherwise stark and minimal flat-roofed pavilion. From a distance the pavilion appears to be filled with a literal fog or steam of uncertain origin, reminiscent of Diller Scofidio + Renfro's Blur Building (2002). As one moves closer, clear streams of material appear to be pouring out of the ceiling, spilling onto the floor. It is not until one has entered the pavilion that the actual material of the spatial fog is revealed as white rope. Large and small rooms are carved into the rope field by adjustments in strand length. A cross section through the pavilion reveals igloolike spaces that, from the outside, contribute to the gossamer atmosphere and, from the inside, produce unexpected pockets of space.

The architects further explain: "By hanging hundreds of white ropes from the pavilion's ceiling, an effect is created where The Cloud is always changing. Visitors moving or a light breeze creates a subtle movement of the ropes, underlining the organic nature of the installation and the immateriality of the space. In Chinese culture, a cloud is an important symbol and a sign of good fortune."[23] In the context of this chapter, it is productive to consider that a project might mimic a natural condition not by using the natural phenomenon itself (e.g., ice, heat, humidity, or light) or by representing that material (like a material that looks like ice or water) but by instead trying to capture an essential, intangible quality of that material. The rope in The Cloud pavilion does not look like condensed water droplets, nor is it made of condensed water droplets, but somehow it captures the delicate, ethereal essence of clouds.

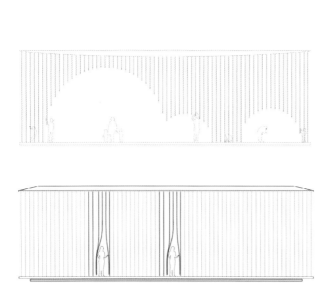

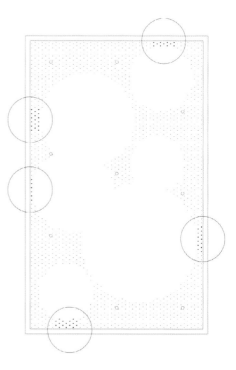

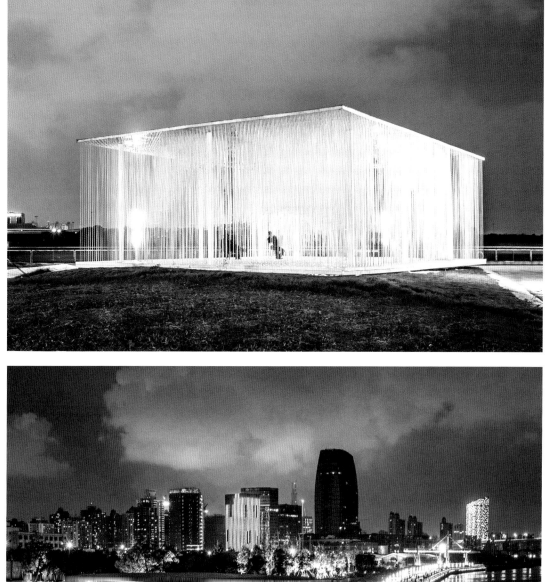

Cloudscapes

Tokyo, Japan, 2012
Tetsuo Kondo Architects and Transsolar
Energietechnik GmbH

The emergence of the term *nanoclimate* parallels the parsing of climatological data along increasingly compact geographic areas.[24] Although its size has yet to be officially defined, it is considered a level of magnitude smaller than a *microclimate*—which is often used to describe areas like neighborhoods or wooded landscapes. Prompted by increasing interest in global climate transformations, nanoclimates reveal the intricate variations that can exist at the scale of a small garden or a room—spaces that may differ markedly from their surroundings.

Cloudscapes is an example of nanoclimatological architecture. Designed by Tetsuo Kondo Architects in collaboration with Transsolar Energietechnik GmbH, it is a small, two-story cube sheathed in transparent plastic. Based on prior experience designing an atmospheric installation within the Arsenale building at the 2010 Venice Biennale, here the team created a stand-alone structure in a recessed courtyard at the Museum of Contemporary Art in Tokyo.

Cloudscapes achieves a startling feat of nano-climatological engineering—effectively "trapping" a cloud within a clear, habitable container. A stair traverses the middle of the space, allowing occupants to experience three different atmospheric strata: a cold, dry layer of air at the bottom; a warm, humid layer in the middle of the cloud; and a hot, dry layer above. As spray nozzles emit a fine cloud generating mist at midlevel, the temperature and humidity within the cube are tightly controlled to maintain the three distinct atmospheric levels.

Although the installation appears hermetic, it is actually designed to respond to its own microclimate. Supported by ultrathin two-inch-diameter (5 cm) pipes, the clear vinyl facade reacts to local changes in wind pressure, propagating exterior forces within while keeping the cloud and its atmospheric layers intact. In this way, what appears to be a detached environment actually maintains a loose connection with the world beyond—a tiny piece of sky brought down to earth.

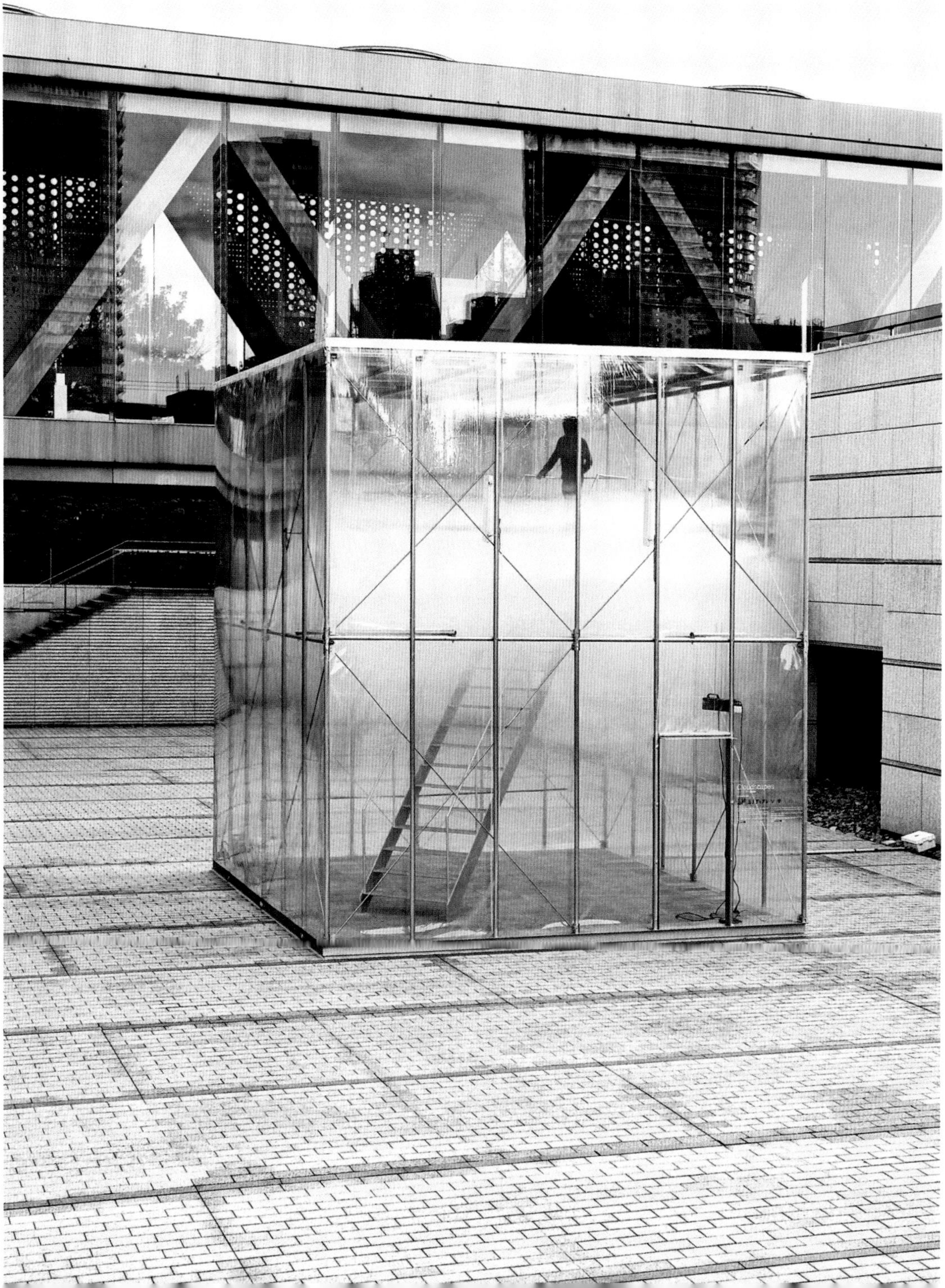

Basel, Switzerland, 2013
Dorell Ghotmeh Tane Architects

A sun pillar is an atmospheric phenomenon that occurs when sunlight is reflected off the horizontal surfaces of millions of platelike ice crystals.[25] Typically produced when the sun is close to the horizon, sun pillars are narrow columns of light that appear to extend sunlight upward or downward in the sky. The collective shimmer of these crystals lengthens the light beam between five and ten degrees from the source, and the light generally assumes the coloration of the sun. Depending on cloud activity and the locations of the crystals, multiple sun pillars can appear. This optical phenomenon also occurs with other light sources, such as the moon, bright planets, or streetlights.

Dorell Ghotmeh Tane Architects' *Frozen Time* project translates the visual experience of sun pillars within an interior environment, bringing visitors into proximity with the glimmering crystals. In this version of atmospheric mimicry, the suspended particles are actually the movement plates of wristwatches. Designed for Japanese timepiece company Citizen and installed at the watch and jewel industry exhibit, Baselworld, the project shrewdly marries the concepts of time and light. The architects hung fifty thousand movement plates on three thousand metal wires, carefully positioning the plates at different angles—with up to thirty possible configurations—in order to heighten the impression of a complex natural phenomenon. They mounted nearly 240 programmable LED spotlights to the ceiling and floor to illuminate the shimmering metal pieces, simulating lower and upper light pillars.

A visually engrossing spectacle, *Frozen Time* employs subtlety and sophistication in its representation of client merchandise, and first-time visitors are often surprised when they discover the true identity of the suspended crystals. Furthermore, the project captures the allure of an evanescent atmospheric phenomenon without being overly literal, freezing it in place for prolonged observation.

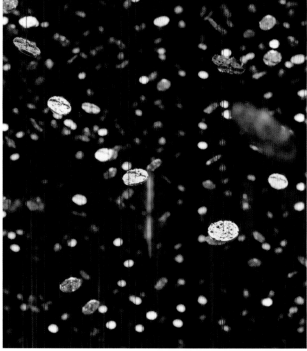

Miami, Florida, 2012
Asif Khan

Parhelia comes from the Greek words *para*, meaning "beside," and *helios*, meaning "sun." Also known as a sun dog, the word describes a phenomenon appearing in the atmosphere when the sun is low in the sky (around twenty-two degrees) and floating ice crystals, oriented horizontally, refract light into a circular halo.[26] Designer Asif Khan was inspired by this rare atmospheric phenomenon when he developed the Parhelia Pavilion for Miami Design Week. It is constructed from over 1.3 million Swarovski crystals and a thin metal frame. An LED light in the center of the pavilion, along with a hole in its roof, provides light that interacts with the crystals to simulate the atmospheric properties of sun dogs.

Parhelia's walls are composed of both clear and "aurora borealis" crystals, which have a special coating to refract light similarly to ice crystals in the atmosphere. Other zones of the wall are kept clear to allow outside light to infiltrate the space. To fabricate the pavilion, individual crystals were hand-formed into honeycomb panels, which were then hung on the pavilion's frame to yield a smooth, unadorned interior atmosphere. Visitors experience the space by ducking under the elevated frame and popping their heads up into the pavilion's cozy interior. Halos projected inside the space fluctuate in size and orientation as the viewer changes his or her position.

Parhelia is a notable contributor to the topic of atmosphere because it so sharply focuses on suppressing physical materials in order to foreground the intangible. In his own words Khan relates that Parhelia "bring(s) people closer to light, make(s) light tangible, make(s) the experience of light something intimate."[27] Like most projects in *Hypernatural*, Parhelia exemplifies a willingness to quiet authorial will in favor of an allowance for natural phenomena to bear the responsibility of providing architectural poesies.

Windswept

San Francisco, California, 2012
Charles Sowers

The Tower of Winds possessed one of the earliest known examples of a weather vane. Built by astronomer Andronicus Kyrrhestes of Macedonia during the first century BCE in the Agora of central Athens, the forty-three-foot-tall (13 m) octagonal structure exhibited a series of measurement apparatuses—including sundials, a water clock, and a planetarium.[28] A bronze weather vane in the form of Triton, son of Poseidon, embellished the top of the building, above a marble frieze depicting the eight wind gods.

A traditional weather vane is simple in its design: a lightweight, directional object is imparted with equal balance yet unequal surface area. Although the center of gravity is located above the pivoting axis, one side has a larger surface area, and this side receives the brunt of the wind's force. The opposite side, which is the location of the pointer, rotates to face into the wind.

Since the Tower of Winds, weather vanes have almost exclusively appeared in a singular, horizontally oriented form at the tops of buildings. For his design of the *Windswept* installation, however, artist Charles Sowers devised a field of vertical wind instruments to map not just the general wind direction but the intricate movements of air across a building facade. Installed on the exterior of San Francisco's Randall Museum, *Windswept* consists of an array of 612 aluminum wind vanes spanning a 35-by-20-foot (11 by 6 m) area. The project required four years to design and construct: Sowers made dozens of prototypes of the aluminum arrows before deciding on the final iteration, and each arrow had to be carefully balanced when installed.

Windswept gives visibility to a natural force that, although we experience it every day, is otherwise unseen. Described by museum visitors as being reminiscent of a field of undulating wheat or a rippling school of fish, the installation demonstrates that a building skin need not merely obstruct the wind—it can also reveal its true form.[29]

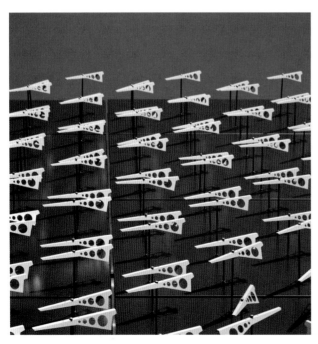

HYDROSPHERE

HYDROSPHERE

In *The Four Elements of Architecture* (1851), Gottfried Semper writes that architecture is composed of four basic elements: the hearth, the roof, the mound, and the enclosure.[1] Semper's "enclosure" is delineated by hung ornamental tapestries that are personally relevant, culturally specific, and flexibly interchangeable. Semper considered this *clothing* of architecture to be far more significant than its structure. Its thin surface contained all of architecture's significance, meaning, and beauty. The Digital Water Pavilion by Carlo Ratti Associati may perhaps be the purest interpretation of Semper's enclosure to date. It uses planes of water as walls. Digitally controlled droplets fall from nozzles in the roof to produce intricately woven planes of water. Like Semper's tapestries, these water curtains change with shifts in use and occupation over time, forming the primary visual vocabulary of the building (see pp 70–71). The structure of the building, along with its conventional roof and walls, are of little consequence; they are there to simply hold up the water.

Originally designed as a tourist information center for the Zaragoza Expo in Spain in 2008, the building now houses a cafe and an informational kiosk. The project deploys some three thousand solid brass solenoid valves, twelve hydraulic pistons, several dozen oil and water pumps, and a camera-operated control system to produce a curtain of water with precisely controlled openings. The sheets falling from the roof can be thought of as low-resolution digital monitors; images, animations, text, or patterns can be visualized just as they are on a computer screen or printed on paper.

How the project uses water as a substance imbued with pattern, shape, and texture is its most noteworthy characteristic. The water is continually changing, sometimes allowing passage, sometimes not, sometimes outlining a room, while at other times defining a passageway or a single wall. The system is temporal and ethereal, constantly reacting to environmental change and the presence of people. For example, if a person walks up to a wall, it might splay open like a curtain to allow for her dry transition from exterior to interior. If a ball is thrown at the wall, a camera might sense its presence and drop a circular opening that allows for the ball to pass through uninterrupted. The presence of a person walking parallel to the building

might trigger a water surface that travels by her side to keep her cool on a hot day. The water might also react to sound, moving in harmony with footsteps, crowd noise, traffic, or music.

The possibilities for water to serve as a reactionary, dynamic building material are endless in the Digital Water Pavilion. Because the material is so shapeless and dynamic, it can be coaxed into new forms endlessly to modify the shape, opacity, and density of the traditional wall. This is the opportunity afforded by partnering with the *hydrosphere*—the liquid water constituent of the planet. While it resists control and is historically considered the nemesis of architects, when it is harnessed as a material, it is perhaps our most dynamic, powerful, and adaptable natural sphere.

Background

Water is an essential ingredient for life, and living organisms depend on water for their continued survival. However, water presents tremendous perils as a destructive force of nature—whether in the form of a tsunami, flood, or body of water harboring pathogenic microbes. As a result, humans' relationship with the hydrosphere has embodied this inherently contradictory pairing of life and death.

Water has long held deep religious and cultural significance for many societies, and its utilization as a resource has transformed the natural landscape, giving form to cities and infrastructure. Despite water's importance, however, its implicit dangers have encouraged its strict control. Throughout architectural history, the hydrosphere has largely been kept at bay; water has been permitted to enter buildings almost exclusively for the sake of convenience (e.g., plumbing). Otherwise, its ability to bring destruction and decay has made it an unwelcome entity. However, recent awareness of the growing global scarcity of freshwater has inspired an alternative approach, inviting architects to incorporate hydrospheric processes within architecture in order to acknowledge and conserve what may be our most underappreciated natural resource.[2]

The evolution of the city is closely aligned with the history of water use. With the emergence of civilization in the Fertile Crescent, Mesopotamian societies developed irrigation by 5000 BCE as a way

roof has functioned primarily as a shield against precipitation. Beginning with simple animal pelts, adobe, or thatch, the roof has evolved over time into a complex system of sloped, impermeable surfaces with an accompanying network of gutters, scuppers, and downspouts, all designed to eliminate water thoroughly and efficiently from a building. This intricate system serves as a kind of extroverted plumbing. In fact, it shares the same basic approach as plumbing in that it directs water intentionally via strategic points and channels to desired locations. Today this strategy extends to the scale of the city: the development of impermeable road surface materials, such as asphalt and concrete, in conjunction with modern gutter and pipe-based sewer systems, has expanded the drainage role of the watertight roof to the extents of the metropolis. One unintended consequence of this approach is watershed imperviousness, which has resulted in reduced aquifer flow, hydrologic cycle disruption, and diminished biodiversity in many parts of the developed world that require groundwater recharge for their ecological health.[5]

to overcome insufficient rainfall for cultivated wild grains and cereals.[3] As the material systems for water conveyance became more robust, humans were able to transport and store water across longer distances and in larger quantities. The resulting water infrastructure—whether a Roman aqueduct, an Indian step well, or a modern hydroelectric dam—has left an enduring mark on the land, constituting some of our most recognizable monuments. Today humanity's attempt to control water on a continental scale represents one of our most impressive—and often environmentally disastrous—engineering achievements.

Control over water is similarly omnipresent within architecture. Plumbing appeared early in the history of building, with evidence of clay pipes used in the Indus Valley by 2700 BCE and in the Minoan Palace of Knossos by 1700 BCE.[4] The latter pumped water to fountains, faucets, and the first flushing water closet. The Romans later developed sophisticated plumbing systems for private and public use, with grand works such as the Baths of Caracalla (216 CE) and Baths of Diocletian (306 CE) in Rome. Fig. 1 Meanwhile, the development of roofing technologies and waterproofing methods served another means of water control: the regulation of the hydrosphere's influence on the building interior. As architecture's first surface, the

Despite the general treatment of water as a substance to be either consumed or eliminated, there are many notable works of architecture that celebrate water, giving it an expanded experiential role. Frank Lloyd Wright's Fallingwater residence (1935), Louis Kahn's Salk Institute (1963), and Tadao Ando's Church on the Water (1988) are three of the most memorable twentieth-century buildings that pay homage to significant contextual water features, establishing strong visual connections between them and interior spaces. Fig. 2 Other works go farther in creating immersive experiences with water: the traversable whirlpool in Philip Johnson's Fort Worth Water Gardens (1974), the lotus pond entrance of Tadao Ando's Water Temple (1991), the aqueous floor of Kengo Kuma's Water/Glass house (1995), and the cavelike pools of Peter Zumthor's Therme Vals (1996) are examples of hydrospheric architecture, inviting visitors to participate in direct, engrossing encounters with water. More recently, appreciation for the dearth of global freshwater has encouraged an increased number of strategies that include water as a primary component of the architectural parti, defying the age-old tendency to simply convey rainwater away from buildings.

Digital Water Pavilion

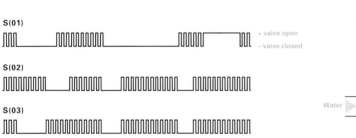

S(01)

+ valve open
− valve closed

S(02)

S(03)

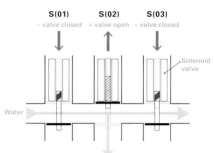

S(01)
− valve closed

S(02)
+ valve open

S(03)
− valve closed

Solenoid valve

Water

A digital processor signals each of the 3000+ solenoid valves. Each is either on (+) or off (−).

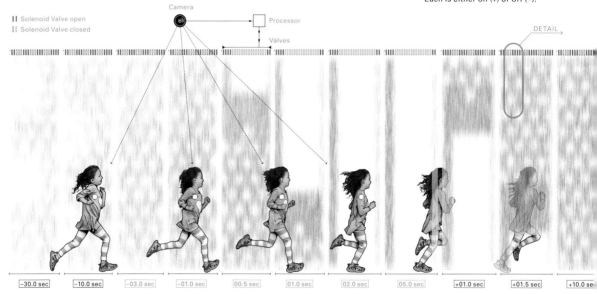

‖ Solenoid Valve open
‖ Solenoid Valve closed

Camera

Processor

Valves

DETAIL

−30.0 sec | −10.0 sec | −03.0 sec | −01.0 sec | 00.5 sec | 01.0 sec | 02.0 sec | 05.0 sec | +01.0 sec | +01.5 sec | +10.0 sec

RESPONSIVE SYSTEM (1)

Gateway: The water pavilion responds to an occupant. The camera registers a child and signals the processor. The system creates a temporary portal. Once the child is through, the fountain returns to its regularly scheduled programming.

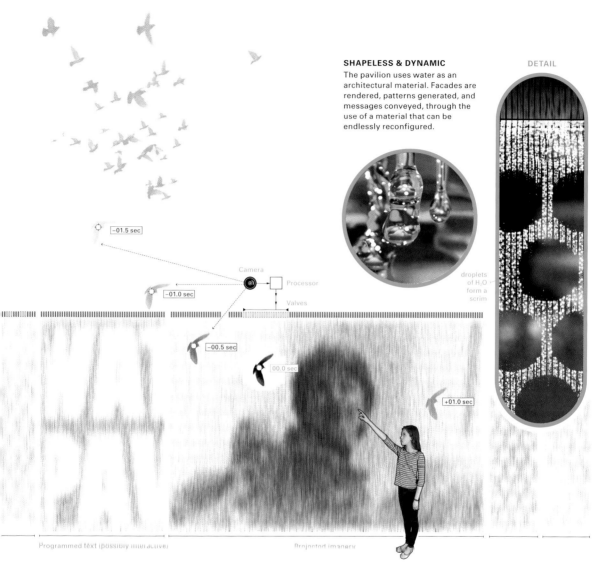

SHAPELESS & DYNAMIC

The pavilion uses water as an architectural material. Facades are rendered, patterns generated, and messages conveyed, through the use of a material that can be endlessly reconfigured.

DETAIL

droplets
of H$_2$O
form a
scrim

Camera

Processor

Valves

−01.5 sec

−01.0 sec

−00.5 sec

00.0 sec

+01.0 sec

Programmed text (possibly interactive)

Projected imagery

RESPONSIVE SYSTEM (2)

Air Drop: The water pavilion responds to an unscheduled occurrence. One of several cameras "sees" a bird approaching. The processesor calculates trajectory and drops a small "hole" to allow the bird to pass through the wall of water.

Material Basis and Behaviors

Water is challenging for architects to manage under normal conditions because it can assume vastly different forms. In a liquid state, it seeks low ground, exploiting material porosity, no matter how small, to achieve equilibrium. As a gas, it is elusive and shapeless, quickly filling any space it occupies. As a solid, it grows in volume, cracking the stoutest materials that attempt to resist its expansion. Entire building material industries are founded on the basic task of controlling water's powerful and damaging forces. However, when viewed as an asset, rather than a liability, water can be leveraged to produce architectural expressions impossible with any other material. To do so, architects and researchers are working to understand the hydrosphere's basic principles, which is not an easy task given that the scientific community still does not fully understand this most basic of earth's compounds. Fig. 3

It cannot be overstated how important water is to life on our planet, or how ubiquitous it is as a material. It is the only inorganic liquid that occurs naturally on earth. While it makes up only 0.02 percent of the earth's total mass, it covers 71 percent of its surface. It is a compound required for almost all living growth and persistence, from respiration to photosynthesis. Organic life on earth is also composed primarily of water. For example, it makes up

two-thirds of the human body's mass, serving as a solvent and lubricant to transport essential nutrients to our cells and carry waste away from them. Water is also essential to erosion and decay. The Mississippi River Delta loses the equivalent of one football field of marshland because of water erosion every hour.[6] Water moves, cycles, builds, and erodes constantly. Through the hydrologic cycle, it undergoes a continuous looping process of evaporation and condensation. Water in the atmosphere cycles about thirty-seven times per year, evaporating from our oceans, lakes, and rivers, falling from the sky as precipitation, then running off the land to start the process over, aggressively shaping our landscape along the way.[7]

As a material, water is unique. It is a chemical compound made of two hydrogen atoms bonded to one oxygen atom. Pure water at room temperature is odorless, tasteless, and nearly colorless. It has the second-highest specific heat capacity of all known substances, which is the heat required to raise the temperature of a substance by a given amount. This is significant because it means that water is not subject to rapid temperature fluctuation, which in turn makes it an effective governor of climatic change.[8] Water is one of the few substances in which its solid form is less dense than its liquid form; this is why ice floats. Water molecules have a bent, asymmetrical shape, providing them with a charge displacement called an electric dipole.[9] This means that one end of the molecule is positively charged, while the other end is negatively charged. Water bonds through a negative-to-positive bonding structure known as hydrogen bonding (as well as through covalent bonding where electrons from neighboring atoms are shared). Scientists note that water *should* actually boil at −130 degrees Fahrenheit (−90°C), making its native form on earth a gas.[10] But because of its unique form of hydrogen bonding, water has the remarkably high boiling point of 212 degrees Fahrenheit (100°C).

In recent work involving hydrospheric research, architects have embraced these unique water properties. Some work directly with pure water's distinct characteristics, like its high surface tension, to produce unconventional architectural surfaces that fluctuate quickly in real-time. Some mix water with other compounds to produce liquid media that perform in unexpected ways. Yet others leverage water's

exceptional visual characteristics, like how it reflects light or responds to wind, to produce surfaces that react to contextual fluctuation in ways never before possible with conventional materials.

Technology

Given the requirement of water for survival, humans developed myriad ways to collect, treat, transport, and utilize water from early times. Industrialization led to a jump in scale for these technologies and ushered in a new paradigm of water-thirsty manufacturing and agricultural processes, as well as colossal civil engineering works. Historian Paul Josephson invokes the term "brute force technology" to describe these approaches, referring to the example of the modern hydropower station as "the culmination of the vision of engineers and businesspeople to transform nature into an orderly, well-oiled machine."[11] This unrestrained manipulation of the hydrosphere, and particularly the insatiable consumption of freshwater, has resulted in the rapid depletion of aquifers. A recent study revealed that 35 percent of the 2005 global population resided in areas with chronic water shortage, and this number continues to increase.[12]

Today scientists and designers are developing alternative technologies that utilize water more efficiently and with less ecological impact. For example, Australian designer Edward Linacre devised a nimble irrigation system called Air Drop, which captures moisture from the air and stores it underground for crop irrigation.[13] Tools such as Stephan Augustin's Watercone, Eric Olsen's Solar Water Tarpaulin, and Vestergaard Frandsen's LifeStraw provide safe, low-impact water desalination and disinfection capabilities in lieu of traditional water treatment infrastructure.[14] Other water purification approaches include University of Washington's SODIS (SOlar DISinfection of water), which uses sunlight to create potable water, and The Living's River Glow, a network of floating pods that serves as a public interface for water quality.[15] Fig. 4 Hydroelectric technologies are also becoming more ecologically responsive. Manufacturer WorldWater & Solar Technologies has developed a series of mobile, off-grid solutions for solar-powered water delivery. Their Mobile MaxPure Freshwater system provides thirty thousand gallons of freshwater per year for less than one penny per gallon and can also generate up to 3.5 kW of solar power.[16] Developed for building infrastructure, Hierve's Hydroelectric Lamps are a novel intersection between plumbing and illumination, converting hydrostatic pressure into energy to power transparent, water-infused light fixtures.[17]

Another significant area of hydrospheric technology development concerns permeability. Scientists are creating new materials based on natural approaches

5. Tunable Material, by
the Wyss Institute at
Harvard University

6. Blob Motility, by Akira
Wakita and Akito Nakano,
Keio University, Tokyo, 2010

to water repulsion and absorption. For example, scientists at Harvard University's Wyss Institute for Biologically Inspired Engineering looked to tears for inspiration in developing a new material that can tune its relationship with liquids by adjusting the size of its micropores.[18] Fig. 5 When a lubricant is added to the adaptive surface in a resting state it becomes transparent and liquid droplets roll off freely. Once stretched, however, the material not only becomes more opaque but also prevents liquid from moving farther—even counteracting gravitational forces. Researchers at the University of Michigan and the U.S. Department of Energy's Brookhaven National Laboratory are developing superhydrophobic surfaces for advanced aerospace and automotive applications.[19] The coatings are composed of nanostructured films that prevent water absorption. Sto AG and Pilkington offer hydrophobic paints and glazing, respectively, that employ the natural sheeting action of rainwater to remove dirt—thus reducing maintenance of building facades.[20] Scientists are also developing superhydrophilic materials for water collection and filtration: researchers at Eindhoven University of Technology and Hong Kong Polytechnic University have created a new treatment that makes cotton fabric superabsorptive, capable of soaking up as much as 340 percent of its own weight in water from moist air.[21] And this research is being applied at an infrastructural level, with a variety of new pervious paving solutions that permit groundwater recharge, as opposed to traditional, impermeable surfaces.

Application

In what was a radical spatial organization strategy at the time, Wright designed a singular, unbroken gallery leading from the public space of the street to the top level of the Solomon R. Guggenheim Museum in New York. According to a definitive biography of Wright, the museum embodied "an architecture that was fluid, plastic, continuous, and has utterly changed our ideas of the nature of space and structure."[22] The grand sloping spiral of the Guggenheim embodied not only Wright's intentions to reflect the intrinsic potential of the plastic medium of concrete but also the fluid character of postwar society. Sociologist Zygmunt Bauman devised the term *liquid modernity* to describe the flexible and inconstant nature of this society, which is characterized by unprecedented opportunity as well as a growing condition of nomadism.[23] Wright and other architects have sought to create a more fluid architecture in acknowledgment of this cultural transformation, with the aim to reduce physical and visual barriers that limit access and programmatic adaptability.

Many contemporary designers and architects embrace fluidity as a central concept, going so far as to use water and other fluid media as principal materials of expression. Their work demonstrates a growing interest in infusing the interactive and evanescent qualities of the hydrosphere within the designed environment. Describing water as "an elemental substance and a natural interface for human beings," Japanese artist and engineer Sachiko Kodama creates dynamic

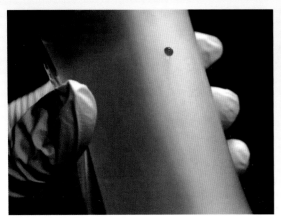

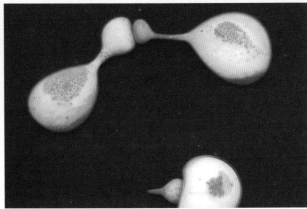

7. Living
Surface, by
B.lab Italia

8. Facade detail, Hungarian
Pavilion, by Tamás Lévai,
Shanghai, 2010

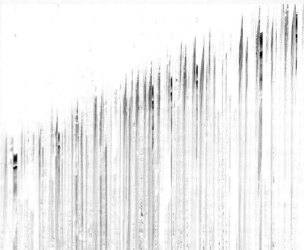

sculptures using ferrofluid—a magnetically charged liquid that, although made with an oil base, conjures a continually morphing, aqueous experience.[24] Interactive textile designer Akira Wakita developed a digital interface based on pBlob, a magnetic fluid controlled by electromagnets and control circuits.[25]
Fig. 6 Design firm B. lab Italia applies interactive fluids to flooring by encapsulating dyed or magnetically charged liquids within resilient polymer shells.[26]
Fig. 7 Other examples that utilize water as a primary interface are NONdesigns' Wet Lamp, an enclosed, water-filled glass fixture that uses water as the electricity-carrying medium; Hara Design Institute and Atelier Omoya's Water Logo, an environmental sign that uses pixelated water drops to form transient words; Fountainhead's SmartFountain, a water feature that responds to visitor body movements; and Frederik Molenschot and Susanne Happle's Solid Poetry, a seemingly nondescript concrete surface that reveals intricate graphic patterns when wet.[27]

Architects also employ water to regulate the interior climates of buildings, since it is an effective medium for mitigating peak temperatures—particularly in dry climates. Grimshaw Architects' British Pavilion for the 1992 Seville Expo boasted a 213-by-59-foot (65 by 18 m) water-drenched curtain wall. Designed as a passive cooling strategy, the continuous glazed surface—unimpeded by protruding

mullions—served as a visually arresting demonstration of evaporative cooling for building visitors.[28] Other projects, such as Tamás Lévai's 2010 Hungarian Pavilion in Shanghai or the University of Arizona's 2009 Solar Decathlon house, utilized water-filled tubes or interior Trombe walls, respectively, as visible conduits for passive thermal regulation.[29] Fig. 8 Increasingly, architects are also joining multidisciplinary teams to tackle large-scale, environmentally focused water-related projects. Examples include Catherine Seavitt and Guy Nordenson's Palisade Bay, a reimagined New York–New Jersey Upper Bay in the wake of climate change–induced flooding and KVA MATx and Tom Leader Studio's RiverFirst project, a proposal to reconnect blighted North Minneapolis industrial corridors with the Mississippi River.[30] As these schemes demonstrate, water is an increasingly vital medium to be considered in projects of any size

Rotterdam, Netherlands, 2012
DUS Architects

Glycerin is required for water to form large, substantial bubbles. With about one-third the surface tension of water, the mixture forms spherical bubbles that would otherwise break under the high surface-tension conditions of pure water.[31] Further, glycerin slows evaporation, which also prevents pure water from maintaining bubbles. The molecular structure of glycerin affects the color and pattern of soap bubbles. They are composed of a hydrophobic end (which repels water) and a hydrophilic end (which attracts water), causing the asymmetrical molecules to reflect light differently and produce iridescent colors. Further, glycerin and water react differently to gravity, resulting in swirling color patterns.

Bubble geometry has informed the structural design work of Frei Otto and others, like PTW Architects and Arup in their design of the Water Cube natatorium for the 2008 Beijing Olympics. But the use of glycerin film as an architectural medium is rare. For good reason: it is extremely temporary. Rather than see this as a liability, however, the Bubble Building exploits the temporal qualities of bubbles as a source of poetic transience and beauty.

The Bubble Building in Rotterdam, by the Dutch firm DUS Architects, is a public outdoor pavilion composed of sixteen hexagonal, shallow pools filled with a thin layer of soap and water. By lifting metal rings that circumscribe these hexagons, membranes of glassy, rainbow-colored film stretch to form temporary pavilion walls. The pavilion grows in complexity as more participants lift the rings, yielding layers of film that catch and reflect light to produce a colorful,

dancing foam in the space. The project virtually disappears when unoccupied. Its "walls" are only momentarily constructed through interaction by its inhabitants. The Bubble Building adopts shapes and spatial characteristics that migrate dynamically over the span of minutes or even seconds.

Worth briefly mentioning here is a related glycerin project called Solace, by artist Nicky Assmann. It relies on sophisticated software, complex mechanics, and an ever-evolving glycerin recipe to yield large curtains of layered translucent color. Unlike those in the Bubble Building, these bubble surfaces are as tall as a single-story building and can last for minutes at a time. Inevitably, the screens burst, creating moments of anticipation and tension impossible to match with conventional architectural materials.

Barcelona, Spain, 2010
Axis Mundi

Water is immediately recognized by the wave activity that occurs along its surface. In physics, surface waves form on water when fluids of different densities intersect, such as water and wind or two different masses of water, causing the propagation of fluid along the interface.[32] These mechanical waves often exhibit interference patterns, which result from the meeting of two or more waves along the same medium. The interference may be either constructive, in the case of waves moving in the same direction, or destructive, in the case of waves moving in opposite directions. Visually, these familiar patterns communicate instantaneous information about present physical conditions—such as wind speed and direction, water speed and direction, the presence of currents, and the nature of subaquatic features.

New York design firm Axis Mundi sought to replicate these patterns in a building facade retrofit for Barcelona-based H₂O, a bottled water company seeking to increase its brand recognition. In a clear example of hydromimicry, the designers analyzed water surface morphologies and their resulting optical effects, selecting a gently rippling pond surface for translation into a new building envelope. They constructed a precise three-dimensional model from a chosen image and traced sections through the model to create multiple wave profiles. The designers then created a new, alterable digital surface by lofting these profiles between one another. By carving out the resulting openings that occurred in the valleys between waveforms, Axis Mundi created windows for unobstructed views. The designers specified this new surface to be constructed out of reflective phenolic composite panels, with minimal joints for maximum visual effect.

The H₂O Headquarters is located in the vicinity of Antonio Gaudí's Casa Milà, an acclaimed work of the highly expressive Catalan Art Nouveau period; thus its water-mimicking skin makes allusions to Gaudí's gently rippling facade. However, if the Casa Milà's exterior is often likened to the rough exposed walls of an open quarry (the building's nickname is La Pedrera), the H₂O Headquarters' facade could be interpreted as referencing the water contained within —a thin, light-reflective surface contrasting with Gaudí's rugged escarpment.

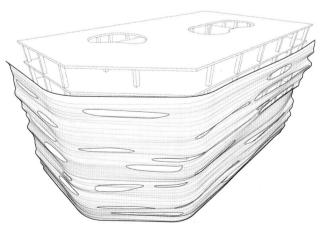

Hydramax

San Francisco, California, 2012
Future Cities Lab

One key advancement in architecture for a more seamless merging of the synthetic and the biological is automated adaptability. Plants and animals persistently monitor their environments and adapt automatically to change. Buildings, on the other hand, traditionally remain unvarying from day to day or season to season. Sure, we can open the windows or close the shutters on a house to accommodate heat waves or windstorms, but this is scarcely an automated response. Hydramax, by Jason Kelly Johnson and Nataly Gattegno of Future Cities Lab, leverages shape-memory alloys and building-scale robotics to yield an environment that organically reacts to daily changes in weather and occupation. The project, a proposal for a new waterfront pier in San Francisco, transforms the hard edges of the existing waterfront into a series of *soft systems* that obfuscate distinctions between building, landscape, infrastructure, and machine.

Hydramax strikes a new, more accommodating relationship with water. Typically, waterfront infrastructure stands in opposition to the dynamic fluctuations of water—tides, waves, and even habitats. It strives to separate land from water and, consequently,

is under constant repair. Hydramax, in contrast, relies on the infiltration of water for its very operation. Programmatically, it consists of aquatic parks, community gardens, wildlife refuges and aquaponic farms. Occupants are faced with water, in one form or another, at every turn. Large feathers on the roof of the structure collect and harvest dense bay fog, converting it to water stored in the building's trusses. To harvest the fog efficiently, the feathers, which are controlled by large robotic arms and sensors, unfurl to optimize their orientation.

While we have seen automated responses at the scale of materials and envelopes, they rarely happen at the scale of building geometry. On the occasions when they have occurred, they have often been in the service of conceptual agendas or metaphors. Hydramax, however, utilizes dynamic building movement to blend with its landscape and to blur distinctions between human and natural ecologies. Its complex, organic movement system is offered in a spirit of reverence for natural forces and with a humble awareness of architecture's role as a backdrop for human activity.

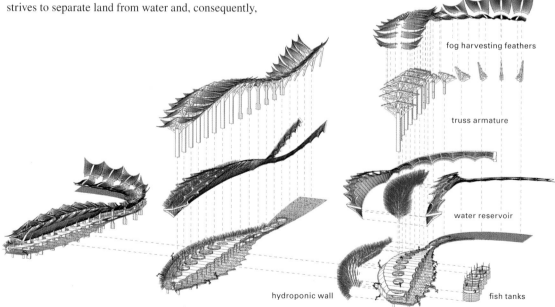

fog harvesting feathers

truss armature

water reservoir

shell + truss + fog feathers

hydroponic wall

primary shell

fish tanks

Rain Room

London and New York, 2012
rAndom International

The Rain Room is an example of hydrodesign augmented by real-time computation. An interactive installation that premiered at the Barbican gallery in London in 2012 and was later presented at the Museum of Modern Art in New York in 2013, the project demonstrates the experiential potency made possible by exerting precise control over a natural phenomenon.

Designed by UK-based rAndom International, the Rain Room is a one-thousand-square-foot (100 sq. m) simulation of a rainstorm in which visitors remain dry, regardless of their location. A grid of spouts dispenses water in a steady cascade over a grated floor below. When occupants venture bravely into the downpour, however, three-dimensional tracking cameras sense their presence and trigger custom software to shut off individual solenoid valves connected to the pipes directly overhead. Bright illumination further enhances the effect by highlighting the droplets against the black background of the surrounding space. As a result, the inhabitants of the Rain Room are able to sense the immediate, powerful presence of rain—its sight, sound, smell, and humidity—without the direct contact of water.

The project originated out of an unexpected marriage between fountain design and printing technology. rAndom extrapolated the operations of ink jet printing—in which a print head controls the deposition of multiple ink droplets with a high degree of precision—to a room-sized water feature. In this way, the grated ceiling of the space effectively becomes a print head for water. Although seemingly simple in its operation, the installation required the development of a highly tuned water management system with pressure regulators that dispense water at a rate that mimics heavy rainfall.

As a simulated environment, the Rain Room exemplifies the aspirations and consequences of human control over nature. The ability to manipulate the weather, particularly in a targeted and precise way, is a nearly inconceivable possibility—yet the notion continues to entice scientists actively pursuing cloud seeding and other climate control approaches. The occupant seeking the cooling effects of the rain, however, becomes a modern-day Tantalus—everywhere she travels, water is just beyond her reach. The architectural implications of the Rain Room are equally surprising: even within this tempestuous void, shelter is accommodated by computation alone, without the need for physical barriers or facades.

Water Cathedral

Santiago, Chile, 2011
GUN Architects

Stalactites are the preserved embodiment of a focused point of convergence between the hydrosphere and geosphere. When water, rich in calcium carbonate and carbon dioxide, seeps into a cave at a sufficiently slow rate, it hangs temporarily from a drip edge in the cave's ceiling. This momentary suspension provides time for the carbon dioxide to escape, and the calcium carbonate is also released—leaving a small amount of solid calcium carbonate behind.[33] Successive drips repeat the process on the surface of the original material, and a stalactite eventually forms.

As researchers at the University of Arizona discovered, stalactites form according to an equation of motion described by fluid dynamics.[34] Regardless of their size, stalactites assume the same shape based on this geometric law of motion. Surprisingly, the scientists found that icicles obey the same morphological equation, despite the fact that they form based on heat diffusion and a rising column of air—a convergence between the hydrosphere and atmosphere.

GUN Architects' *Water Cathedral* embodies both the form and process of this motion equation in an outdoor architectural installation. Although the project does not represent the literal, physical materialization of stalactites or icicles, it illustrates the gradual downward movement of water using geometrically self-similar cones (with pyramidal bases) made of fabric. Designed as a cooling shelter for summer visitors, the *Water Cathedral* was installed in Santiago as the winning entry for the 2011 Museum of Modern Art Young Architects Program International. Supported from steel frames and tension wires, the artificial stalactites were conceived to release water held within internal plastic reservoirs at different speeds, collectively generating a temperate microclimate within the public plaza below. The architects varied the distribution of the tapered structures along the linear site, allowing visitors to regulate their desired temperature and humidity levels based on the density of the stalactites.

Philips Design describes their Microbial Home project as "a domestic ecosystem that challenges conventional design solutions to energy, cleaning, food preservation, lighting, and human waste."[1] How? By employing the services of millions of microbes. The project challenges a commonly held belief that we must eliminate all bacteria in our environment. Instead, it relies on bacteria to convert and transmit energy from one household function to another, and then back again.

Revealed at Dutch Design Week 2011 in Eindhoven, the Microbial Home project is a collection of conceptual apparatuses that transforms the home into a testing lab for carbon-neutral living. The project is a reaction to the current imbalance between natural and human-made resources on our planet. It focuses on the traditionally neglected problem of waste, seeking to filter and reuse all forms of household refuse—such as garbage, sewage, and wastewater.

The Microbial Home, which was developed as part of the Philips Design Probes program, is less an architectural proposal than a system of interdependent appliances—a biological machine that operates as a cyclical domestic ecosystem within the framework of a residential structure (see pp 90–91). The eclectic mix of devices—which includes a biodigester kitchen island, an evaporative cooler and dining table, and an urban beehive—makes aesthetic references to the science lab and the retro-futuristic steam-punk movement. The main point here, however, is not a particular visual language but an alternative vision of domestic resource management.

"Designers have an obligation to explore solutions which are by nature less energy-consuming and non-polluting," says Clive van Heerden, Philips Design's senior director of design-led innovation: "We need to push ourselves to rethink domestic appliances entirely, how homes consume energy and how entire communities can pool resources."[2]

The science behind the project is fascinating, effectively demonstrating an ethic of mutualism between architecture and biology. The central component of the system is its biodigester kitchen island. In it, biogas is produced as a by-product of a particular strain of bacteria feeding off household waste. In turn, this gas is burned for cooking, heating, and lighting. Sludge left over from the process can safely be used as garden compost. Microbes like bacteria play the central role in virtually all the Microbial Home's systems. Bioluminescent bacteria are used to light the house, fungi are used to convert plastic into a medium that grows edible mushrooms, and human microbes are collected by an apothecary to monitor the health and well-being of the home's occupants.

The Microbial Home design team asserts that the electromechanical age in which we currently live is responsible for the environmental issues with which we are now dealing. To address these issues, we must enter into a new biotechnical era. What emerges is an architecture that interfaces with biology in a completely new way, one based not on resistance but on compliance, not on control but on accordance.

Background

Over the course of history, humanity's interactions with the microbial world represent a wide range of responses. This is largely due to three factors, the first of which is the diverse nature of microorganisms, which include desirable as well as harmful species. For the purposes of this chapter, we consider prokaryotes, which consist of archaea and bacteria, and eukaryotes, which include algae, fungi, protozoa, and microscopic animals such as planarians. We also touch on viruses—although these are excluded from the field of microbiology, since they are regarded to be nonliving. The second factor is the broad geographic presence of microorganisms, which exist practically everywhere on earth—including extremophiles, which inhabit extreme contexts, such as deserts or the deep sea.[3] The third factor concerns the mysteries surrounding microorganisms that, because of their largely invisible nature (many microbes are not observable by the naked eye, although a few are macroscopic), were not officially discovered until the seventeenth century.[4] Since then, humans have exhibited curiosity, fear, and a desire to control the microorganic world. Increasingly, however, we are adopting a collaborative approach in our relationship with microorganisms.

Humanity's attitude toward the microbial sphere has roughly paralleled its consideration for nature in general: as an enigma and a threat, but also a boon. Prior to the scientific revolution, microorganisms were a mysterious force. After their discovery, they

were largely regarded as dangerous and undesirable given the fact that pathogens—or infectious microorganisms—were (and still are) one of the leading causes of human death.[5] Over time, however, science has revealed the benefits offered by microbes—which play a fundamental role in digestion and food chemistry—including their role as powerful agents in energy harvesting and environmental remediation.

Despite microbes' tiny size, they have influenced the development of the designed environment. One of the most notable stories of the city's connection to microbes is the Broad Street cholera outbreak of 1854. Although microorganisms had been observed via the microscope nearly two centuries previously, their link to disease was not yet understood. Doctor John Snow analyzed the burgeoning cholera cases occurring within the badly affected Soho district of London, tracing their connection to a public water pump used by the diseased residents. Fig. 1 Snow's discovery influenced the development of modern sanitation infrastructure, as well as the fields of epidemiology and public health.[6]

The architectural typology most influenced by microorganic considerations is the hospital. Early hospitals were associated with religious institutions and often planned around open-air courtyard spaces. The miasma theory of disease transmission by poisonous

air—although erroneous—was highly influential until the late nineteenth century.[7] The colonnaded pavilion model exemplified by Pierre Gauthier's Lariboisière Hospital in Paris (1853) had become a popular way to improve health via access to fresh air and light. Fig. 2 However, with Louis Pasteur's 1861 germ theory of disease and the Industrial Revolution came a more mechanical, systemized approach to medicine, and by the mid-twentieth century hospitals exhibited deep floor plates and robust air-handling infrastructure. These mechanized buildings were designed for efficient control over pathogens at the expense of disconnecting their inhabitants from the positive benefits of the natural environment.

Humankind's attempt to control deleterious microbes has been accompanied by its aim to harness beneficial ones. Yeast, for example, plays a critical role in baking and brewing—practices that began as late as 6000 BCE. Other food-related processes, such as yogurt, cheese making, and pickling, involve the use of microbial agents. The development of the scientific fields of biotechnology and biochemistry parallels the increased utilization of microorganisms to produce fuel, treat sewage, clean pollution, and even fight disease—advantageous functions that would have been unimaginable for the first discoverers of microscopic life.

Microbial Home

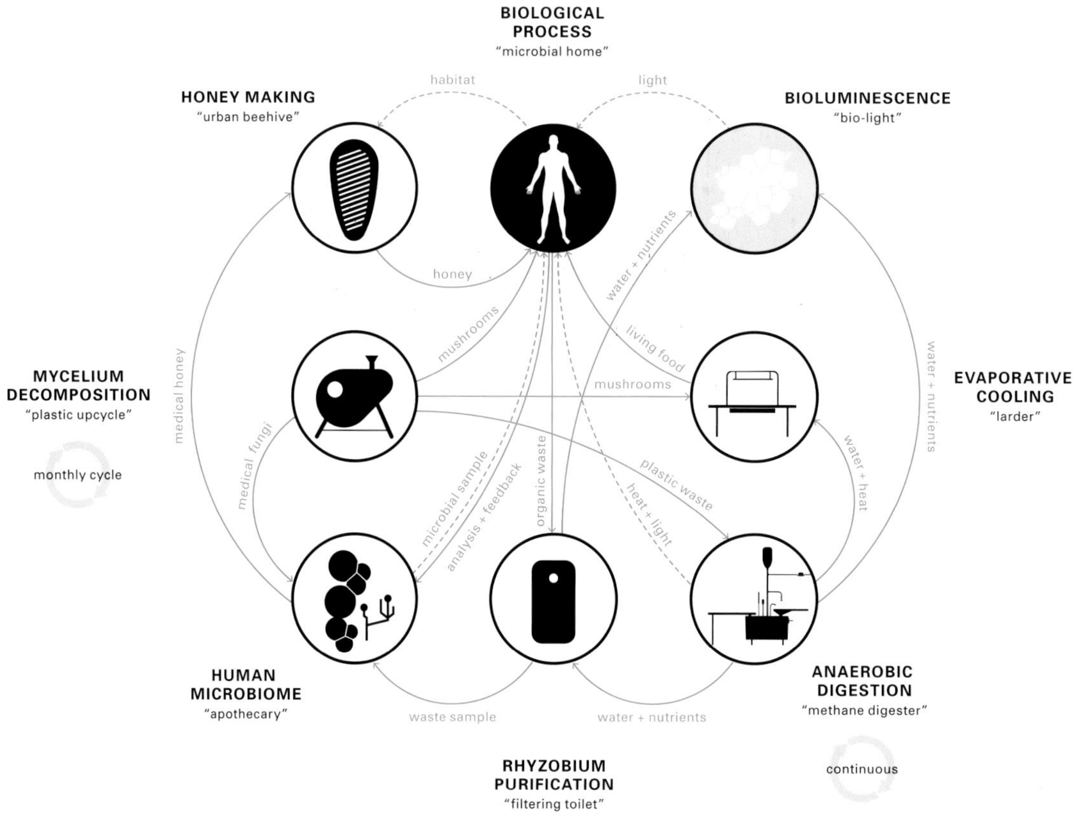

BIOLOGICAL PROCESS
"microbial home"

HONEY MAKING
"urban beehive"

BIOLUMINESCENCE
"bio-light"

MYCELIUM DECOMPOSITION
"plastic upcycle"

monthly cycle

EVAPORATIVE COOLING
"larder"

HUMAN MICROBIOME
"apothecary"

ANAEROBIC DIGESTION
"methane digester"

continuous

RHYZOBIUM PURIFICATION
"filtering toilet"

habitat

light

honey

water + nutrients

living food

mushrooms

mushrooms

medical honey

medical fungi

water + nutrients

water + heat

microbial sample

analysis + feedback

organic waste

plastic waste

heat + light

waste sample

water + nutrients

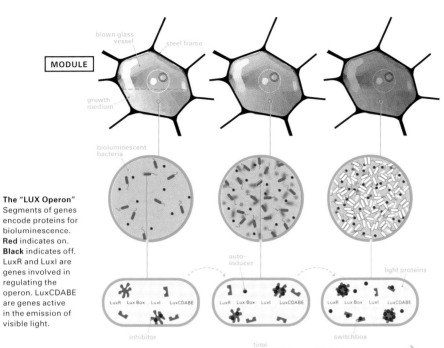

MODULE

blown glass vessel
steel frame
growth medium

bioluminescent bacteria

The "LUX Operon"
Segments of genes encode proteins for bioluminescence. **Red** indicates on. **Black** indicates off. LuxR and LuxI are genes involved in regulating the operon. LuxCDABE are genes active in the emission of visible light.

auto-inducer

LuxR Lux Box LuxI LuxCDABE
LuxR Lux Box LuxI LuxCDABE
LuxR Lux Box LuxI LuxCDABE

inhibitor

light proteins

switchbox

time

"Quorum Sensing"
A system of stimulus and response that correlates to population density. Some bacteria use this mechanism as a trigger for the production of bioluminescent proteins and light.

Biological Light
As population density increases, the concentration of auto-inducers eventually overwhelms the inhibitors. This acts as a trigger that switches genes on to produce bioluminescent proteins.

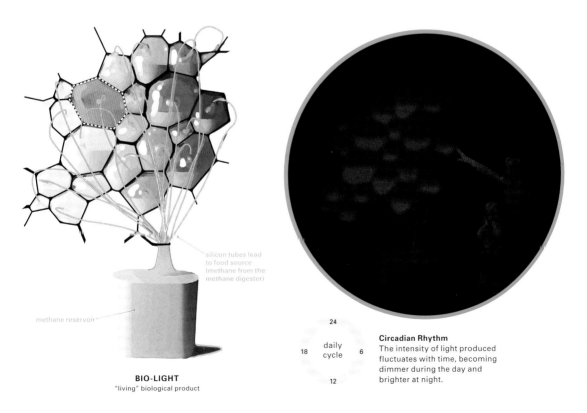

silicon tubes lead to food source (methane from the methane digester)

methane reservoir

BIO-LIGHT
"living" biological product

24
daily cycle
18   6
12

Circadian Rhythm
The intensity of light produced fluctuates with time, becoming dimmer during the day and brighter at night.

Material Basis and Behaviors

We typically consider bacteria harmful, associating them with disease and illness. Fig. 3 The same is true with protozoa, fungi, and other organisms that make up our microbial biosphere. In reality, however, these organisms are essential to life. Consider the human stomach. Scientists refer to the collection of microbes in our gut as a *microbiome*, an ecosystem of diverse organisms essential for proper food digestion.[8] Babies born by C-section are more susceptible to illness early in life because the C-section is a relatively pure, germ-free procedure compared with vaginal delivery where babies are exposed to bacteria. The exposure to bacteria immediately upon birth is an important process that jump-starts the development of illness-fighting stomach microbes. From the earliest stages of life, we need microbes to survive.

Microbes fall into one of two categories: eukaryotes and prokaryotes. Prokaryotes are the simplest types of cells, preceding the evolution of eukaryotes. They are organisms without cell nuclei or other membrane-bound organelles; most are unicellular. An organelle is a subcellular structure that has a specific function (like an organ in the human body). Bacteria are the only example of prokaryotes. Eukaryotes contain a cell nucleus and are organized into complex structures by internal membranes; most are multicellular. Examples include human cells, algae, and fungi. Prokaryotic and eukaryotic cells also have

similarities. Both are enclosed by outer cell membranes (called plasma membranes), and both use DNA to store their genetic information. Interestingly, viruses are neither prokaryotes nor eukaryotes because they lack all the characteristics of living things aside from the ability to reproduce. By studying the basic structures and life principles of these biological building blocks, architects are developing research that challenges disciplinary convention.

Principles that emerge from the study of plants and animals can similarly be observed in microbes (structure and function, photosynthesis and respiration, evolution and natural selection). But microbiologically inspired work differs from plant- and animal-inspired work in three unique ways. First, it often invests in phenomena that occur at a very small scale. This can yield materials-based research, work that explores invisible, sensorial phenomena rather than visual agendas or work that enlarges the invisible to render it newly perceptible. Second, it is often embedded within a larger "host" organism, striking a symbiotic relationship similar to that between microbes and their hosts. These relationships range in character from commensalistic to mutualistic to parasitic. Third, it often favors community over the individual. When microbes are studied in relationship to larger organisms, it is apparent that the larger organisms are really just a collection of smaller living beings. Take, for example, the human body. We are made up of only 10 percent "human" cells. The other 90 percent of us is composed of microbial organisms working through a collective ecosystem to break down food, fight off disease, purify blood, or clean the air we breathe.[9] That the design of a whole building can grow unpredictably from the purposeful development of a material or component-based rule set is owed to our observations of how microbiology contributes to macrobiology.

Technology

Humans have employed microbes as a resource since prehistoric times, although the existence of microorganisms was not proved until the seventeenth century with the invention of the microscope.[10] Scientists such as Lazzaro Spallanzani, Louis Pasteur, and Robert Koch then became focused on the detrimental effects of microbes—particularly pathogens—and developed methods to prevent spoilage as well as the spread of disease. Today, science still maintains a sharp focus on disease prevention; however, it has also come to appreciate the wide range of processes that transpire in the microbial world. Increasingly, scientists are developing innovative ways to work with microorganisms to address important technical and environmental challenges.

A thorough understanding of microbes' capabilities begins with an analysis of their forms, structures, and metabolisms. The material composition of the smallest life forms, and the way in which microbes process material flows, remains an important topic for microbiologists and other researchers. For example, scientists at the French National Center for Scientific Research are studying the glass skeleton of the diatom.[11] As it grows, the diatom absorbs silicon atoms present in ocean water and assembles them into sophisticated glass structures. The form of marine algae not only dispels the myth that glass is a human invention but also demonstrates that glass does not require embodied energy for its fabrication. Researchers are attempting to emulate this and other microbial assembly methods in various nanotechnological applications. Harvard materials scientist Joanna Aizenberg, for example, has created a variety of microstructures such as crystal blooms made by the kind of bottom-up growth found in mollusk shells, biological concrete in a microgrid of sponge-like strands, and hydrophilic smart coatings that can change color with humidity.[12] Other researchers are experimenting with protocells, which are simple chemical models of living cells that—although technically not living—exhibit lifelike properties, such as response, growth, and self-assembly.

Designers and manufacturers are also devising ways to grow microorganic materials at a macroscale. Ecovative Design creates mycological biocomposites, which are made from mycelium and agricultural waste, for insulation, packaging, and product design applications.[13] After discovering various ways in which to control root growth within prefabricated molds, designers Merjan Tara Sisman and Brian McClellan employed fungi to create the Living Room Project, which consists of a prototype chair and pendant light made from the mycelial roots of mushrooms.[14] Designer Eric Klarenbeek and scientists from

the University of Wageningen went a step farther, employing digital fabrication and living materials in the creation of their Mycelium chair.[15] Fig. 4 After 3-D printing a bioplastic shell with a straw core, the team grew fungus within the frame of the chair, creating a solid yet lightweight material.

Scientists view microorganisms as a fundamental tool for environmental remediation. Anaerobic microbes are commonly used in waste treatment, as are mycorrhizal fungi employed to clean up contaminated soils. Northwestern University researchers have also developed methods to remediate nuclear waste using colonies of *C. moniliferum* algae, which deposit the radioactive isotope strontium-90 safely into crystalline structures called vacuoles.[16] Scientists have also discovered ways to biodegrade waste plastic safely using fungi and ultraviolet light, as well as to transform organic waste into new plastic with genetically modified microbes. In addition to converting materials, microorganisms can be used to heal existing structures. For example, a Newcastle University research team developed a genetically modified microbe that can rebuild cracks in concrete.[17] When a fissure forms in the material, the bacteria swim to the bottom of the crack and create a mixture of calcium carbonate and microbial glue that effectively patches the concrete. This bacterial patch ultimately cures to the same strength as the surrounding material— a living patch for a nonliving substance.

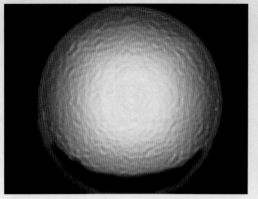

Energy is another principal area for microbe utilization. Microalgae, which are highly efficient in their conversion of sunlight into biomass, are increasingly cultivated for biofuels as well as food products. Cambridge scientist Paolo Bombelli and designers Alex Driver and Carlos Peralta employed algae in the development of a series of energy-harnessing biophotovoltaic (BPV) devices—from algae-powered table lamps to giant algae-coated lily pads that aggregate to form offshore power plants generating five to six watts per square meter.[18] Algae have also been used to make more efficient batteries by replacing the electrode binder material in lithium-ion batteries with alginate. Other microbes can produce energy without sunlight: Stanford University researchers developed a microbial battery made from exoelectrogenic microbes that convert sewage into energy, and Bielefeld University scientists created a battery that converts bacteria directly into energy.[19] And a team of University of Wisconsin researchers employed *E. coli* bacteria to produce their own light: their Biobulb—or microbe-powered lightbulb—is an enclosed ecosystem that functions as a self-powered light source.[20] Fig. 5

Application

The challenge when considering microbiology as an analogue for the development of architecture is that there are vast differences in scale between the two fields of study. Architects have confronted this incongruity in a number of unexpected ways. Generally, the strategies fall into three categories: reactive, communal, or sensorial.

Reactive work considers microbes at the material scale, resulting in architectural surfaces that actively push back on environmental forces like erosion, darkness, or pollution. Through the development of material assemblies that incorporate particular species of microbes themselves, researchers have been able to leverage the reactive capabilities of biology to produce self-healing structures, self-illuminating fabrics, and pollution-scrubbing walls. One such project is by the Structural Technology Group at the Universitat Politèctica de Catalunya, which is developing a multi-layered concrete panel system designed to support the growth of mosses, fungi, and lichens. Fig. 6 The so-called biological concrete is based on the use of two types of cement: conventional Portland cement and magnesium phosphate cement (MPC), which has a slight acidity and supports biological growth. In the system, which is the focus of the PhD thesis of Sandra Manso, materials are combined to form four layers: a waterproofing layer, a structural layer, a bioreceptive layer that aids the growth of organisms, and a reverse waterproofing layer that retains water for the plants. Although not yet commercially available, the innovative product promises several benefits, including carbon dioxide reduction via the use of organisms, mitigation of the urban heat island effect, and applicability for existing structures.

Communal work involves the study of microbe behavior in groups, investing not necessarily in what the biology does but in how it operates. Rule-based systems determine how a collection of small, simple parts act in harmony to yield large, complex

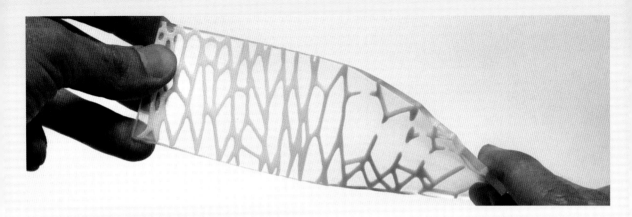

organisms like material assemblies, entire buildings, or even urban systems. Such systems might embed themselves into a normative or existing condition where a commensalistic, a mutualistic, or a parasitic relationship might be struck. The Bio Computation project by David Benjamin uses bacteria growth as a model for growing architectural skins with distinct and precisely mapped material properties.[21] Fig. 7 Through observing growth behavior of different kinds of bacteria in a petri dish, digital algorithms model similarly manufactured synthetic materials that combine vastly distinct properties along the cross section of a single sheet of material. For example, a single component might combine the characteristics of structure and transparency across a single composite, a feat that would conventionally require multiple materials attached to one another mechanically.

Sensorial work leverages the invisible and ethereal dimensions of microbes to present an architecture of immateriality. The office of Diller Scofidio + Renfro has produced numerous examples of this. As an experimental practice, the office's work often considers the imperceptible and sensorial dimensions of architecture. In the Art of Scent exhibit at the Museum of Arts and Design in New York, the office chose to eliminate all visually defining elements and instead privilege an assortment of scents to define space.[22] Simple sculpted wall depressions invited gallery visitors to experience different scents, which were paired with sound and light projections. This produced a project defined exclusively by immaterial components (light, sound, and smell) as opposed

to the material ones (brick, wood, or steel). As with many of the projects featured in *Hypernatural*, the Art of Scent resides at the intersection of multiple spheres (in this case, the microbial sphere, hydrosphere, and atmosphere). However, it is referenced here to demonstrate the profound impact that microbial-scale materials can have on our perception of space.

BIQ House

Hamburg, Germany, 2013
Splitterwerk Architects and Arup

Splitterwerk Architects and Arup collaborated with Colt International and the Strategic Science Consult of Germany to create the world's first bio-adaptive facade. Composed of microbe-infused glazing panels, the system utilizes living microalgae to harvest solar power while providing shade. The new envelope was installed on the *BIQ (Bio Intelligent Quotient) House* project in Hamburg for the 2013 International Building Exhibition, and produces energy for the building in two ways: by capturing solar thermal heat and by generating biomass for harvest. Because photosynthesis drives microbial growth within the liquid-infused glazing panels, more intense sunlight accelerates algae germination and biomass production. As a result, windows that would normally receive the most solar glare from an interior perspective become more effective shading devices.

Named the *SolarLeaf*, the bio-adaptive facade of the *BIQ House* is a form of vertical *algaculture*, or algae farming. Algaculture most often cultivates microalgae, such as phytoplankton or microphytes (as opposed to macroalgae or seaweed), for a variety of needs, including fuel, food, fertilizer, dyes, and bioplastics. Microalgae are particularly desirable because of their superior energy conversion compared with that of higher-level plants.[23] The SolarLeaf employs a version of autotrophic growth, in which water-submerged algae convert sunlight and carbon dioxide into glucose and oxygen. In this system, liquid nutrients are pumped together with carbon dioxide via a constant loop through the vertical panels. Although the surface algae are sensitive to direct sunlight, the algal culture located immediately behind the exposed layer responds well to this condition and grows quickly as a result. Meanwhile, the heated water in the window panels is used as hot water or to augment the building's geothermal system. Once the algal culture is ready for harvesting, it is removed from the system and either transferred to the building's biogas fermentation plant or stored for food or pharmaceutical use.

Although an early prototype, *BIQ House*'s bioreactor facade is a compelling demonstration of bioengineered architecture, in which living materials are employed as a fundamental component of building performance. Producing 150 kWh/m² per year in heat energy and 30 kWh/m² per year in biomass, the SolarLeaf skin is estimated to have offset the building's carbon dioxide emissions by 6 tons per year, with an energy conversion efficiency ratio of 38 percent for solar thermal heat and 10 percent for biomass.

▲ Detail view of bubbles in algal solution

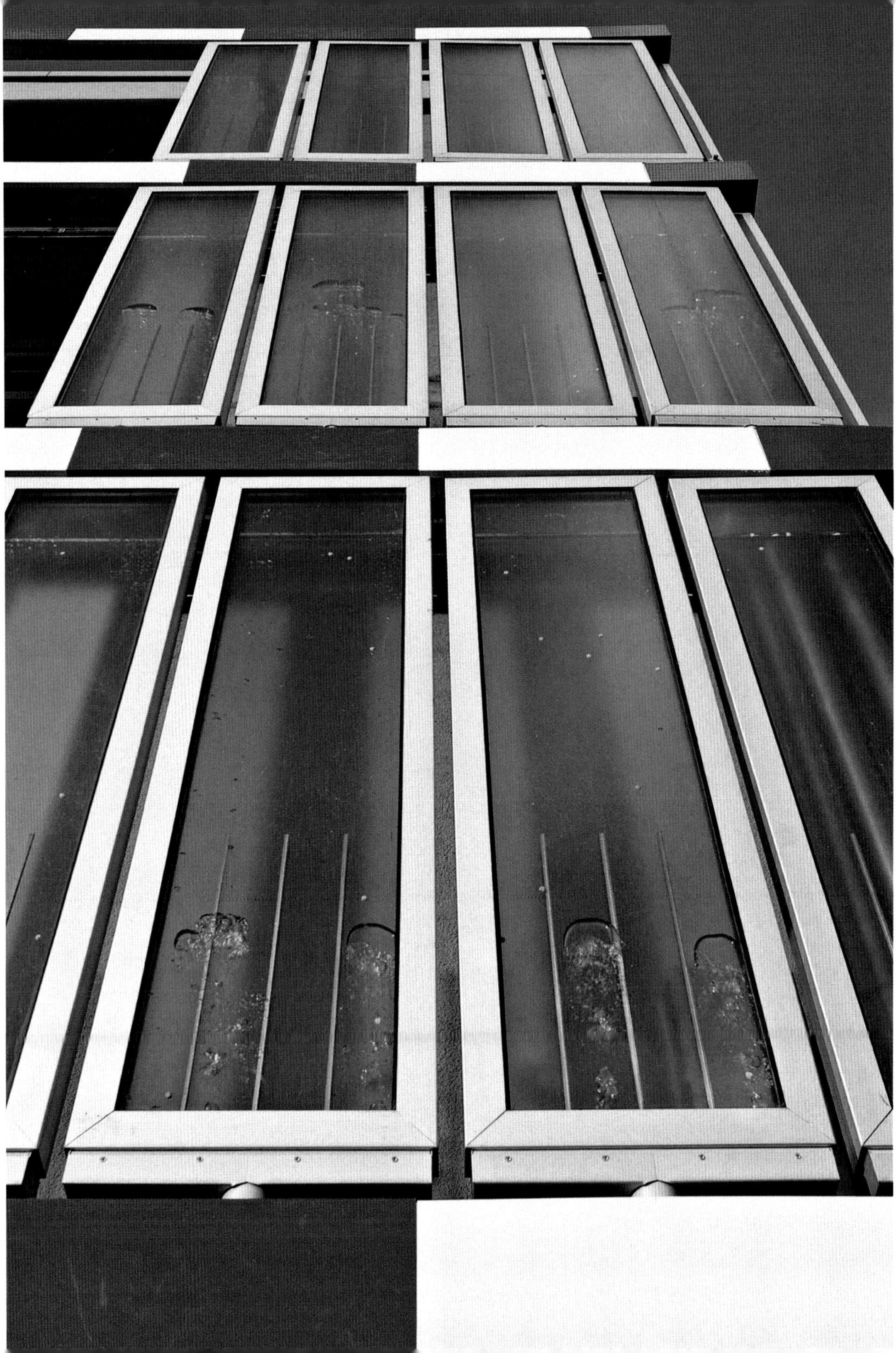

Branching Morphogenesis

Los Angeles, California, 2008
LabStudio

Biology and architecture can converge in remarkable ways. Branching Morphogenesis grew out of a unique collaboration between architect Jenny Sabin, of Cornell University's Department of Architecture, and biologist Peter Lloyd Jones, of the University of Pennsylvania's Department of Pathology and Laboratory Medicine, who together form the interdisciplinary studio LabStudio. The project is a spatial diagram representing various stages of lung endothelial cell growth. Each layer of the piece, referred to by the design team as a *datascape*, is a visualization of a time-lapse of cells as they branch and change in relation to a matrix in which they are placed. Installed in the SIGGRAPH 2008 Design and Computation Galleries, visitors were encouraged to walk around and through the various layers of the environment to understand how cell growth generally and self-organization specifically work in a more visceral and spatial way.

Branching Morphogenesis is designed by a process through which cell-growth geometry is captured, layered, and connected. It is, in this way, biomimetic. However, the project's real contribution to the discourse outlined in *Hypernatural* is that it demonstrates how a set of simple rules and a very limited palette of materials can yield unfathomable intricacy, complexity, and beauty. The piece itself is composed of nothing more than seventy-five thousand

zip ties. Its complex network of branching tubes and crossing volumes is the result of a process by which two-dimensional replicas of cell layers are simply interconnected, point to point. The rules and materials are quite easy to understand, but the resulting architectural construct is visually and spatially complex. The project demonstrates how a component-based architectural system can develop into a networked, responsive system that—like an organism composed of millions of "dumb" cells—can adapt in real-time to environmental fluctuation, automatically and without the need for input from a central brain.

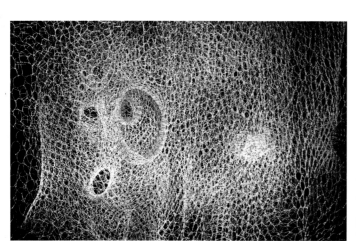

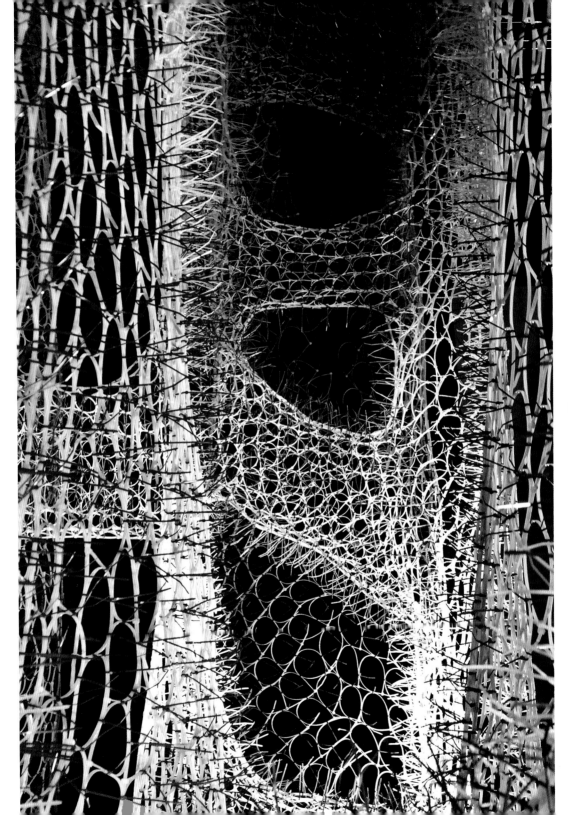

Dune City

Prototype (Sahara Desert), 2008
Ordinary Vis

Disciplinary boundaries within the natural sciences have often curtailed investigations into the interactions between different domains. An example is the relationship between the geosphere and biosphere. As soil interaction experts have pointed out, the significance of interchanges between geological processes and biological organisms has only recently been acknowledged.[24] Bio-soils scientists at the University of California, Berkeley, study methods to reshape soils using biological materials, advocating the ability to improve soil health for agricultural, structural, and environmental purposes.

Based on this research, architect Magnus Larsson developed an ambitious proposal to reduce desertification in Africa by deploying sand-solidifying microbes. For the Green Wall Sahara initiative to curtail desert encroachment, Larsson proposed seeding the sand with *Sporosarcina pasteurii*. This microbe is able to calcify sand via biological cementation, a process in which the bacteria are combined with urea—which serves as a source for nitrogen and energy—causing it to precipitate calcium carbonate after releasing the by-products of dissolved carbon and ammonium (ASM). As a result, sand can be transformed into sandstone, making a much more solid terrain on which protective vegetation may be planted. According to Larsson, the process requires at least one week of ground saturation to produce a habitable structure.[25]

The original version of Dune incorporated the morphology of tafoni—smooth, rounded voids created by cavernous weathering. Although this phenomenon is an erosion process typically seen in intertidal areas, Larsson proposed it as an additive approach to structuring the dunes, providing concave pits that are conducive for thermal cooling and water storage. Larsson collaborated with Alex Kaiser to create the subsequent iteration shown here, which exhibits a collective settlement based on angular tafoni geometries.

In a seemingly insuperable case of the desert being used against itself, uninhabitable sand seas are interrupted by the sheltering borders of microbe-crafted architecture. Despite being an early prototype with outsized aspirations, Dune demonstrates how a vast landscape may be altered by a microscopic agent, effectively conquering the extra-large with the extra-small.

Radiant Soil

Paris, France, 2013
Philip Beesley

Radiant Soil is a suspended, responsive ceiling system that profoundly challenges a number of commonly accepted architectural physiognomies. First, it is deliberately fragile and flexible—unlike buildings, which are commonly constructed to be robust and permanent. Second, it is kinetic and responsive, where buildings are unaware of environmental fluctuation and remain monolithically constant in the face of change. Third, it is dispersed and networked, behaving like an organically decentralized swarm, rather than the hierarchical collection of inert, disconnected materials that make up most buildings.

Designed by Canadian architect and professor Philip Beesley from the University of Waterloo, *Radiant Soil* is biological in the most elemental meaning of the term: it behaves like biology. In appearance it is decidedly otherworldly: a mix of chemistry lab componentry, exposed medical plumbing, and alien metallic foliage. Installed in an exhibit called Alive/Envie at the Espace EDF Fondation in Paris, the piece responds in real time to the movement and proximity of people by lighting itself along LED-lined arteries, moving its biomechanical fronds to generate air currents and releasing unique odors into the air through its scent-emitting glands.

While the project exudes a poetic ethos, and in its current incarnation is not beholden to traditional programmatic necessity, it has profound implications for a new dialogue between humans and their built environments. What the project addresses are biological needs often ignored by architecture; needs we commonly fulfill through experiencing nature. If what we relish from these environments are the smells, tactility, textures, and movement of our surroundings, then *Radiant Soil* meets "programmatic" needs that our buildings have hardly recognized up to now.

Xylinum Cones

Dublin, Ireland, 2013
Hülsen and Schwabe

The Xylinum Cones project by Hülsen and Schwabe presents a strategy for growing geometric building blocks from living bacterial cellulose. Cellulose is a material found in plant cell walls and vegetable fibers, such as cotton. It is also used in the production of paper. Bacterial cellulose, however, is different from the plant-based variety and is characterized by its higher strength, moldability, purity, and its ability to hold more water.[26] The production cycle of each unit is about three weeks during which time it is dried and removed from a suspended armature. While the units are currently informed by the shapes and tiling patterns of reptile scales or flower seeds, they could take on any shape, depending on the geometry of the mold. Hülsen and Schwabe speculate that the units could be developed into viable alternatives for roof tiles or wall cladding.

Like many of the projects in *Hypernatural*, Xylinum Cones calls into question the relationship between the hand of the designer and the natural forces leveraged to produce a material or building. To what degree do architects dictate the shape, color, texture, and size of their work, and to what degree are these characteristics informed by the natural processes used to produce the work? If architecture is evolving into a discipline where materials are grown rather than manufactured, how much of the decision-making process is handed over to nature?

Hülsen and Schwabe state that "the main motivation of Xylinum Cones is to prove the reproducibility of organically grown objects, but also to find a balanced level of geometric precision and organic diversity."[27] The project aspires to make the production cycle of a naturally formed material completely transparent. It accepts the irregularity caused by unpredictable cycles of biological growth and reproduction. While the form of each cone is nearly identical in its current design, one could imagine a scenario in which the formwork is less constrained and the balance between control and variability is shifted slightly to prioritize the voice of the bacteria in determining the units' final outcomes.

▼ Bacterial cellulose occupying suspended molds

Microbial Biosphere

BOTANICAL BIOSPHERE

BOTANICAL BIOSPHERE

In a remote field at the foot of Mount Arera on the outskirts of Bergamo in northern Italy lies a natural cathedral called Cattedrale Vegetale, by Giuliano Mauri. This breathtaking project is a monument to the redefinition of what it means to be an architect. Rather than design, draw, detail, and construct the fabric of the building itself, the artist has envisioned scaffolding that will be used to define the footprint of the cathedral. It will rot away, leaving an open, airy, spiritual space on which the handprint of its designer will be evident, but no trace of human-made material will remain.

The cathedral is built of 42 columns that form a church nave. Traditional local techniques of weaving and lashing connect about 1,800 spruce trunks and 600 chestnut tree branches with 19,685 feet (6,000 m) of hazelnut twigs to form the structural lattice on which the project will grow. Hornbeam saplings were planted at the base of each column and will mature to form a natural roof across the cathedral. The structure occupies 6,997 square feet (650 sq. m), is more than 90 feet (27 m) long and, nearly 80 feet (24 m) wide, and ranges in height from 16 feet (5 m) to nearly 70 feet (21 m). In fifteen years the supporting structure of the cathedral will decay, and the hornbeams will grow to form an organic space of worship. Open on all four sides, the structure was conceived of by Mauri as a place of passage: of silent, unmoving contemplation.[1]

Cattedrale Vegetale serves as a poignant introduction to the potential transformational influences that plant biology can impart on architecture. Like other projects in *Hypernatural*, Cattedrale Vegetale represents a resistance on the part of the designer to heavy-handed authorship. It instead leverages behavioral knowledge of biology, allowing the designed artifact to emerge from a set of understood biological tendencies (see pp 110–11). Precision and craft are displaced. No longer is the building itself an engineered work of joinery and material exactitude. Rather, precision and craft have migrated to the predesign phase of the work. It is only through a carefully researched understanding of an organism's exact reactionary patterns that the designer can embark on envisioning a set of approximated outcomes. Through a willingness to accept this range of outcomes, which are dependent on issues like rainfall, soil composition, temperature, and sunlight, the designer sets into play an ecological choreography. The surprising outcomes that ensue are the very sources of architectural delight.

Background

The relationship between humans and plants has evolved, making a gradual transformation from dependency to interdependency. Because of their pivotal role as oxygen producers, plants are responsible for our existence as well as our continued survival. Plants provide the bulk of our sustenance and have been a primary source for our clothing, shelter, and medicine. Thus our dependency on plants—from prehistory into the foreseeable future—is clear. Over time, however, plants have also come to depend on *Homo sapiens*. This reciprocal reliance is based on our gradual redesign of the plant kingdom to satisfy the needs of agriculture, urbanization, and industrialization. As a result, much of what was wilderness is now under direct human supervision, and many plants have been modified such that they rely on us for their own reproduction. Today, our relationship with plants continues to change, as indicated by an increased awareness of the importance of biodiversity, controversies over genetic engineering, and an intensified focus on renewable resources.

Cellulose, the primary ingredient of plants, provides the material basis for many animal species' livelihoods. Its versatility as a resource presents an opportunity to determine the most appropriate means for its allocation. Reyner Banham expresses the cellulose dilemma in his parable of a primitive tribe that discovers a campsite replete with fallen timber.[2] Two possible uses of the wood exist: the tribe can build a shelter (material) or make a fire (energy). According to Banham, the "ideal" tribe would allocate its timber resources in proportion to its particular needs for protection or warmth. Architect Luis Fernández-Galiano emphasizes the significance of this decision for architecture: "Construction is nourished by flows, combustion by deposits. One feeds on our profits, the other on our thermodynamic capital. The two strategies are perfectly differentiated, yet one excludes the other only when they compete for the same resources."[3]

The primitive hut that emerges from the former strategy represents one of architecture's legendary origins. The shelter drawn by Charles Eisen for

Marc-Antoine Laugier's *Essay on Architecture* depicts a structure made from living trees and repurposed tree limbs—an additive, nestlike approach to building that contrasts with the subtractive, cavelike form of early underground chambers.[4] Fig. 1 As mentioned in the Hydrosphere chapter, Gottfried Semper proposed that the wall first emerged in the form of a woven mat or carpet—another cellulose-based architectural origin.[5]

Given that botanical materials decay, few records remain of humankind's original plant-based structures. However, these material strategies are documented in stone buildings that reveal the translation of timber construction techniques into a more enduring substance. The transubstantiation of plant-based architecture—as well as plants themselves—into non cellulosic materials marks one of the earliest recorded forms of biomimicry. The appearance of palmette decorative motifs and the embodiment of acanthus leaves in the Corinthian capital are notable examples of botanical translation into architecture. Such an approach may be seen throughout architectural history, culminating more recently in the sophisticated floral reliefs designed by architect Louis Sullivan.

Agriculture and the industrialization of plant-based resources are significant human endeavors that have profoundly altered the global landscape. The long-held paradigm of civilization existing in opposition to nature has dissolved, based on the realization that there is little nature left unaltered. Instead, former wilds have been transformed into agroecosystems, marking the conversion from untouched nature into commoditized terrain. Fig. 2 In *Industrialized Nature* historian Paul Josephson discusses the rapid deforestation of the planet, projecting that the current rate of timber consumption will eradicate earth's tropical rain forests within a century.[6] However, bio-based industry experts argue that biomass is too important a material to squander, as indicated by discussions of a resurrected carbohydrate economy.[7] The more likely outcome will be an increased investment in renewable resources (e.g., forests or croplands) resulting in a more intensely planned landscape.

Material Basis and Behaviors

There are two fundamental characteristics of plants that need to be considered in relation to the built environment. First, a plant produces food from its surroundings through photosynthesis; such organisms are known as autotrophs. Second, plants are primarily static. These two characteristics are interrelated. Plants must generate their own food from water, air,

Botanical Biosphere

Cattedrale Vegetale

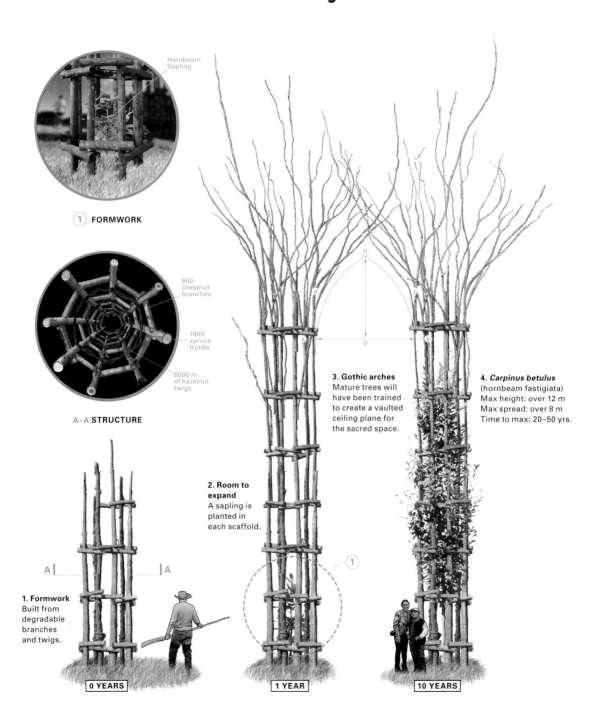

1 FORMWORK

Hornbeam Sapling

A–A STRUCTURE

600 chestnut branches

1800 spruce trunks

6000 m of hazelnut twigs

3. Gothic arches
Mature trees will have been trained to create a vaulted ceiling plane for the sacred space.

4. *Carpinus betulus*
(hornbeam fastigiata)
Max height: over 12 m
Max spread: over 8 m
Time to max: 20–50 yrs.

2. Room to expand
A sapling is planted in each scaffold.

1. Formwork
Built from degradable branches and twigs.

0 YEARS

1 YEAR

10 YEARS

The Hornbeam has an erect, upward sloping limb structure, and its foliage vigorously regenerates when pruned. This makes it ideal for hedges, topiary, and in the case of the Cattedral, architecture.

B–B FASTIGIATE TREE

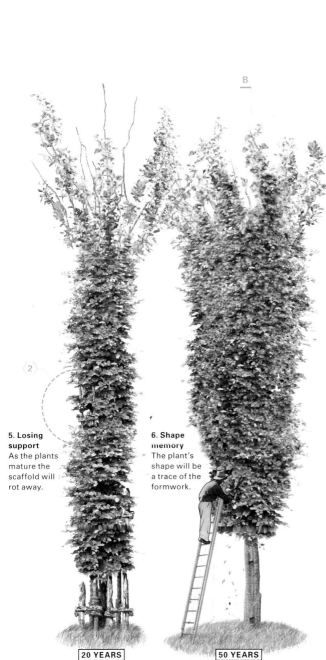

After 15–20 years the forms will rot away, leaving plants as building elements

② **PLANNED OBSOLESCENCE**

5. Losing support
As the plants mature the scaffold will rot away.

6. Shape memory
The plant's shape will be a trace of the formwork.

20 YEARS

50 YEARS

100 YEARS

A PLACE OF PASSAGE

and sun because they cannot move (or perhaps they do not move because of how they produce their food). These qualities render plants immediately relatable to architecture: like plants, architecture is stationary (except, under certain circumstances, where, like plants, buildings move in place to track the sun or to accommodate for wind direction), and, further, architecture is increasingly asked to produce its own energy.

The growth and persistence of plants may help contextualize how plant biology specifically informs architecture. These terms respectively refer to how a plant changes shape and size over time and how a plant converts sunlight, water, and air into food and energy. A plant's primary mechanism for persistence is photosynthesis, which is a process by which a plant converts light energy into chemical energy. In this process, carbohydrates are synthesized from carbon dioxide and water: essentially, photosynthesis is the production of sugar, and glycolysis is the process by which those sugars are broken down to be used as energy. This is life's essential energy recycling process.

The precise mechanisms by which plants grow and persist capture the interests of designers primarily because, as mentioned above, plants are similar to buildings. Plants, like buildings, have circulation systems, foundation systems (their roots), structural systems, and are for the most part immobile. Fig. 3 Architects examining plants are attracted to their capabilities to react, in real time, to accommodate changing contextual conditions. Evident in the examples that follow, growth and persistence represent the two primary directions of research for designers interested in plant biology. Growth morphologies offer models for structural systems, material assemblies, and novel programmatic relationships, while persistence characteristics offer strategies for climatic adaptation, reaction to changing light, humidity, and wind levels, and methods for generating energy in unconventional ways.

Technology

Although humanity has continually utilized plant-based resources, the Industrial Revolution ushered in an era of intensified exploitation and control. Demand for mass-produced goods encouraged the standardization of modular components with predictable characteristics—particularly within building construction, which was transformed by the development of engineered lumber. These products have often been designed to suppress the intrinsic characteristics of natural materials, such as anisotropy or decay. However, many scientists and manufacturers are now seeking ways to emphasize—rather than counteract—the inherent qualities of botanical resources.

Another recent change in perspective relating to plant-based technologies concerns the notion of a material hierarchy in technological evolution. Throughout history, technologies have often appeared in plant materials to be later superseded by more advanced tools made from nonrenewable resources. This phenomenon is evident in the transition from wood clubs to metal axes, from timber bridges and dams to steel- and concrete-based infrastructural works, and from natural resins to synthetic plastics. Today, however, a more sophisticated understanding of bio-based materials and a renewed emphasis on renewable resource development invalidate the presumption that plant-derived products are technologically inferior to their nonrenewable counterparts.

The resurgence in plant-based technologies is apparent in many fields, including construction, aerospace, and computing. For example, firms such as Waugh Thistleton Architects and Michael Green Architecture advocate the construction of high-rise buildings made of wood. Waugh Thistleton's nine-story Murray Grove (2009) building in London is the world's tallest habitable building made of timber, and Green's 90-foot-tall (28 m) Wood Innovation and Design Center (2014) in Prince George, British Columbia, is the tallest contemporary wood building in North America.[8] Both structures make use of innovative cross laminated timber (CLT) panels that act as load-bearing walls and slabs, effectively replacing much more carbon-intensive steel or concrete frames. Fig. 4 The U.S. Forest Products Laboratory is developing wood-based nanomaterials in the form of cellulosic nanocrystals that exhibit transparency, low weight, and a strength superior to Kevlar fiber.[9] The researchers envision this technology being applied to make clear composite windshields and reinforced glass. Other wood-based examples include Aerocork, a biocomposite alternative to aircraft polymer panels, and a carbon-sink computer made of wood.[10]

In addition to wood, other renewable resources are also being rapidly developed into innovative products. Seaweed, for example, is now actively cultivated for building insulation and sheathing, and soybeans are now commonly used to make inks as well as formaldehyde-alternative glues.[11] Bioplastics made from soy, corn, switchgrass, kenaf fiber, and other plants are rapidly gaining ground over their petroleum-based polymer counterparts—and the global bioplastics market is predicted to expand at a brisk 24 percent compounded annual growth rate.[12] Less energy-intensive or resource depleting than synthetic polymers, bioplastics are now offered for a wide range of uses. Examples include whey-based film that replaces pervasive ethylene vinyl alcohol (EVOH) materials, a pineapple and banana fiber composite as strong as Kevlar, dandelion-derived rubber that may be substituted for latex, and grass-based thermoset resins that supplant toxin-filled, synthetic versions.[13]

Botanical materials are also proving their worth in the burgeoning field of digital fabrication. Mcor Technologies, for instance, offers paper-based 3-D printing using selective deposition lamination (SDL) technology, which produces models from many A4-sized sheets of paper with adhesive in between each layer.[14] The process not only provides new capabilities, such as full-color, full-bleed, and lifelike modeling, but also promises 3-D printing at 5 percent of the material cost of current methods. Scientists are also developing 3-D printed food using hydrocolloids, which are gel-like solutions such as agar consisting of particles dispersed in water.[15]

Like their algae-based counterparts, plants are also the primary subjects of renewable energy research. Many scientists view plants' ability to photosynthesize sunlight into chemical energy as a potential solution for our own accelerating energy demands. Investigations include both the morphology as well as processes involved in photosynthesis in an effort to devise more efficient solar cells. Researchers at Northwestern University, for example, analyzed the light-scattering capabilities of leaf cells in order to devise a new geometric arrangement for a polymer-based solar cell and were able to surpass previous thermodynamic thresholds as a result.[16] Based on the discovery that leaf cells frequently repair themselves in the presence of damaging sunlight, Massachusetts Institute of Technology scientists developed synthetic chloroplast cells capable of reoccurring self-assembly.[17] Meanwhile, researchers at Georgia Tech created a solar cell using a nanocellulose substrate

5. Nanocellulose Solar
Cell, by the Georgia
Institute of Technology

6. Double living root
bridge in East Khasi,
India

from trees—thus using a plant-based material for a plant-derived function.[18] Fig. 5 Other energy-related efforts include a battery made from the wood fibers of yellow pine trees, self-cleaning solar windows, and Bio-LEDs, which consist of trees implanted with gold nanoparticles to make them fluoresce at night, thus potentially eliminating the need for street lights.[19]

Application

A diverse array of projects based on our plant-based biosphere challenges long-held assumptions about how buildings are designed, built, and preserved. Green roofs, walls, and other sorts of living surfaces, for example, suggest an architecture of indeterminacy, one composed partially of steel and concrete, but also of living matter that continually changes. Such work is shaped by criteria that lie beyond the control of the designer. For example, buildings might change appearance seasonally or annually, depending on rainfall or temperature fluctuation. Foliage might serve as an intelligent shading mechanism, growing to block light in the summer and then dying off to allow for the passage of light in the winter. Hydroponic systems can dynamically change the temperature, acoustics, or air quality of an interior environment. In each case, as living materials substitute for traditional ones, architects sacrifice control in exchange for systems that are more responsive and, in many cases, offer a startlingly novel aesthetic language.

One recent project to incorporate plant biology this way is the Active Modular Phytoremediation System by CASE (Center for Architecture, Science, and Ecology).[20] It uses a custom-fabricated armature to grow plants, forming an interior green wall that cleans and filters air, and reduces the heating and cooling load on a building's mechanical system. The project offers an elegant example of the symbiotic relationship that architects are just beginning to explore between the made and the natural.

Some researchers are developing full-scale environments grown from plant material: structure, skin, foundation, and all. Others are fabricating environments composed of building blocks designed to decay and disappear. Both types of work suggest a new perspective on temporality in architecture; sometimes a short, predetermined lifespan is precisely what a client or circumstance calls for. While temporary architecture is not new, the notion that impermanence might result in a building that wilts away can only be attributed to growing interest in the relationship between architecture and plants.

Poetically elegant examples of structures grown from plants are the Meghalaya Living Bridges in India made from the roots of rubber plants. Fig. 6 These amazing structures are produced by first extending hollowed-out betel nut tree trunks over river beds as guidance systems. The thin roots of rubber trees are coaxed through these armatures and subsequently take root on the opposite sides of the crevasses they

are bridging. As the rubber trees mature, their roots thicken and intertwine to form robust structural trusses. While these bridges can take up to fifteen years to grow, they can last for hundreds of years and can span up to one hundred feet (31 m).[21]

Of course, architects are also motivated by the responsiveness of plant biology to environmental fluctuation and have begun to incorporate similarly responsive systems into the skins of their buildings. Dynamic shading systems—like the kinetic roof in the Aldar Central Market (2014) in Abu Dhabi, by Foster + Partners and Hoberman Associates—are influenced by plants like the *Mimosa pudica*, or "sensitive plant."[22] In such projects wall or roof transparency is transformed from 100 percent on an overcast, cooler day to 0 percent on a sunny, warmer day. Other systems dynamically adjust a wall surface's color, reflectivity, or acoustic properties, to align more precisely with the fluctuating needs of a building's inhabitants. New sensing technologies and an increasing availability of mechanically and materially dynamic materials allow for building surfaces to be similarly adaptable to both internal and external fluctuation.

The Air Flow(er) project by Andrew Payne of LIFT architects exemplifies this bio-inspired approach to surface design.[23] Fig. 7 Air Flow(er) is an active wall

system that reacts to ambient room temperature by opening or closing itself automatically. To develop the system, the architects first researched the thermostatically responsive system of the yellow crocus flower. This plant is composed of petals with two layers of cells, where one expands more than the other in cold temperatures. This differential allows the plant to quickly open and close its petals in response to temperature fluctuation. Air Flow(er) similarly adjusts its level of ventilation through the use of a shape memory alloy that is highly sensitive to temperature.

Los Angeles, California, 2012
DOSU Studio Architecture

Bloom illustrates the emulation of botanical behavior in nonbiological materials. Designed by architect Doris Kim Sung, Bloom is a twenty-foot-tall (6 m) open-air pavilion clad in gleaming bimetallic strips— a composite skin designed to shape-shift with changes in temperature. Bimetals are made of two types of sheet metal with contrasting coefficients of thermal expansion and are commonly used in thermostats and thermometers. In the presence of direct solar radiation, the exposed material expands at a faster rate, causing the laminated sheet to curve upward.[24]

Although bimetal transformation is based on a physical effect unrelated to biology, the phenomenon resembles solar-responsive behaviors found in plants. Some plant movements align with the diurnal cycle, in what is called circadian responses. The oxalis leaf and velvet leaf, for example, both open during the day and close at night—exhibiting an awareness of changes in light and temperature.[25] In similar fashion, the fourteen thousand bimetallic strips cladding the Bloom pavilion demonstrate clock-dependent feedback, and they curl and flatten with the presence and absence of sunlight, respectively. Rather than regulate biochemical activities or express genes, however, Bloom's circadian response is directed toward temperature regulation for pavilion occupants. To this ends the bimetal strips provide additional shading and openings for ventilation during the peak hours of solar intensity.

The impetus for Bloom came from Sung's interest in the capacity of architecture to adapt for human benefit, rather than the common requirement that occupants adapt to buildings' environmental limitations. Sung's recognition that plants commonly respond to changing environmental stimuli, coupled with the fact that bimetals exhibit behaviors similar to this phenomenon, results in a compelling design application that portends a promising future for responsive architecture.

Echoviren

Gualala, California, 2013
Smith | Allen

The most biological characteristic of *Echoviren*, a project by Smith | Allen located in the Gualala redwood forest in Northern California, is that it was conceived to eventually wilt and disappear. Enriching this poetic quality, which will not manifest for decades, is a host of other biologically motivated characteristics, giving rise to the project's shape, surface quality, materiality, and program.

As the world's first full-scale, 3-D printed architectural installation, *Echoviren* stands ten feet wide by ten feet deep and eight feet tall. It was conceptualized as a graft within the redwood forest, a space of contemplation framing one's view to the canopy above through a geometry of forced perspective. To produce the project's five hundred uniquely shaped components, seven 3-D printers ran continuously for two months. Those components, made of a translucent, milky white plastic, quickly snapped together on-site, shortening installation time to four days.

Smith | Allen designed the surface of *Echoviren* in reaction to biological site research. The pavilion's perforation pattern is a hybrid of morphologies found in *Sequoia sempervirens* cells at the microscopic level and in sequoia bark itself at the macroscopic level. The piece is designed to simultaneously be *of* the forest, through its geometry and surface pattern, while standing in stark contrast to the forest through its distinctly synthetic material and striking luminosity.

This project most notably challenges architecture's relationship with the natural environment through its built-in obsolescence. Made of a plant-based PLA bioplastic, *Echoviren* will decay into the forest floor in thirty to fifty years, at which time it will become food for the growth of new organisms. Along the way, it will take on a life of its own, one that cannot be predetermined by its designers: birds will nest in its holes, which perfectly simulate the space between a tree limb and its trunk; moss, algae, and vines will grow along its surface, rendering its perfectly white surface in mottled tones of green, brown, yellow, and gray; and as its base begins to erode, where it is the most saturated from continuous rainfall, perhaps a wall will collapse, creating space for a gopher den or a foxhole.

This acknowledgment of a life cycle, along with compliance to change, is *Echoviren*'s true contribution to the discourse surrounding architecture's new relationship with biology. In the development of its work, Smith | Allen has given control over to nature, but has anticipated change as an active participant in the design of that work. Since Roman architect Vitruvius, we have traditionally valued architecture that is strong, withstanding, and permanent (*firmitas*).[26] Projects like *Echoviren* directly challenge this assumed quality. What if architecture was instead developed from the perspective that construction is the first phase in a long life of change, growth, decay, and death? How might this challenge the ways in which all buildings are designed and how they interface with the natural environment?

Yeosu, South Korea, 2012
Atelier Brückner + Knippers Helbig
Advanced Engineering

The GS Caltex Pavilion, known as the Energy Field, consists of an inhabitable structure surrounded by a forest of artificial plantings. Architecture firm Atelier Brückner designed the project for CG Caltex, a Korean energy company, for the World Expo 2012 in Yeosu, South Korea. The pavilion features an angular, mirror-clad structure encircled by 380 tall hollow tubes made of glass fiber–reinforced plastic (GRP). Collectively, the 60-foot-tall (18 m) poles represent a rice field at an exaggerated scale, and its artificial blades of grass translate the power of coastal winds into movement. The synthetic grove thus serves as an outsized metaphor for an iconic renewable resource.

The engineers, Knippers Helbig, sought to emulate the resilience of natural grasses and designed the tapered poles to sway in moderate breezes yet maintain structural stability in the event of a typhoon. To make the translucent blades, glass fibers were wound around removable conical steel forms. The desired stiffness was achieved by altering the density and diameter of the fibers along the poles' length—and the result is a varied wall thickness between 0.16 and 0.31 inches (4 and 8 mm), and a change in diameter from 8.66 inches (220 mm) at the base to 2.56 inches (65 mm) at the top. At night, the artificial grasses are illuminated from within by LED chains, and touch-sensitive poles trigger color changes in their neighbors, emanating waves of light throughout the energy field.

Visitors initially confront this artificial thicket without much understanding about what lies within. To reach the interior structures one must traverse a field of gravel in which the poles are planted, thus inviting a process of discovery. The building itself is clad in shimmering chrome, obfuscating its contents with the reflection of its surroundings. In this way the pavilion playfully blurs the boundaries between architecture and landscape, as well as object and field, while also providing an exuberant interpretation of botanical performance in a synthetic medium.

Orleans, France, 2013
Achim Menges with Oliver David Krieg
and Steffen Reichert

The history of the industrialization of timber is a study in the exertion of control over a natural material. The demand for standardization, predictability, precision, and efficiency in mass-produced lumber has resulted in heavily modified products that bear little resemblance to their source substance. This is due to the fact that wood—although a remarkably practical and beneficial resource—possesses unpredictable and imprecise characteristics that contradict the systematizing aspirations of the industrial project. Wood is both anisotropic, meaning it behaves differently in different orientations, as well as hygroscopic, meaning it tends to absorb moisture from the air. These are unacceptable qualities in many standardized building components—resulting in the use of laminates (plywood) and resin-based composites (particleboard) to eliminate the negative effects of anisotropy and hygroscopy, respectively.[27]

As a counterstrategy, architect Achim Menges created the HygroSkin, a so-called *meteorosensitive pavilion* designed to celebrate, rather than eradicate, wood's inherent idiosyncrasies.[28] Part of the permanent collection of the FRAC Centre Orleans, the one-room, timber-based structure has wooden apertures that open and close based on the relative humidity of the surrounding air.

HygroSkin was inspired by spruce cones, which open and close based on changes in humidity, in contrast to the cell pressure–based transformations seen in other plants. Because the movement is enabled by the material itself, this passive, moisture-driven process requires no energy or additional mechanisms. This strategy runs in direct opposition to traditional industrial logic, which prioritizes the aggregation of technical components propelled by outside energy sources.

Despite HygroSkin's seemingly rudimentary approach—eschewing sophisticated, active systems in lieu of simple, passive materials—the pavilion is a precisely calibrated meteorological instrument that is based on years of study concerning the behavior of responsive veneer-composites. Its predisposition toward material effects instead of mechanical processes suggests that its operations will also be more predictable than traditional automated solutions. As the surrounding weather changes, so does the HygroSkin: its delicate wood petals curl and straighten with fluctuations in the atmosphere.

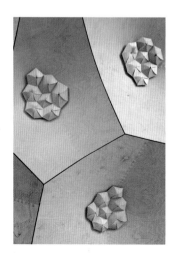
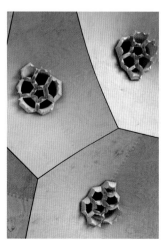

◄ Climate responsive apertures, shown closed and open

Raspberry Fields

Northern Utah, United States, 2010
Jason Payne of Hirsuta LLC

Although this building draws analogies to animal hides and bearskin rugs, it is intentionally included in this chapter on plant biology. Like several other projects in *Hypernatural* (Neri Oxman's *Silk Pavilion* or Guiliano Maure's *Cattedrale Vegetale*), it relies on a key behavioral property of a biological material and generates difference and effect through a strategic leveraging of formal specificity.

Raspberry Fields is a proposal for the renovation of an existing barn structure from the early 1900s built in northern Utah. Designer Jason Payne observed that the existing wood shingles on the barn curled over time at different rates according to the orientation and exposure to sun, wind, and water. In his proposal he adds onto the existing building and reclads it in wood shingles similar to those with which it was originally covered. However, the new shingles are intentionally designed wrong and installed improperly. The four-by-twenty-four-inch (10 by 61 cm) shingles are left unfastened at the bottom, and the grain of the wood is oriented horizontally rather than vertically. Both of these unusual detailing strategies encourage a premature aging of the shingles, revealing another difference between the new and the old. As the shingles curl, a brightly stained underside is

exposed, resulting in what the designer calls a series of bipolar differences: between the top of the shingles and their underside, and between the characteristics of the north and the south facade.[29]

Raspberry Fields is of particular interest because it identifies a biological material (wood) and a property of that material (its tendency to curl over time), and then it upends our expectations of how one would utilize that material architecturally. Rather than resist the material's inherent tendency to deform over time, as is commonly practiced in most conventional architecture, this project accommodates and even celebrates the material's instability. This strategy, which represents an ethic of tolerance over resistance, is a central tenet to hypernatural design. By working with natural systems, rather than against them, and by partnering with biology, rather than battling it, there begins to emerge a paradigmatic shift in architecture where our built inhabitations participate in the messy, dirty reality of our context, and the distinctions between what is natural and what is artificial are upended.

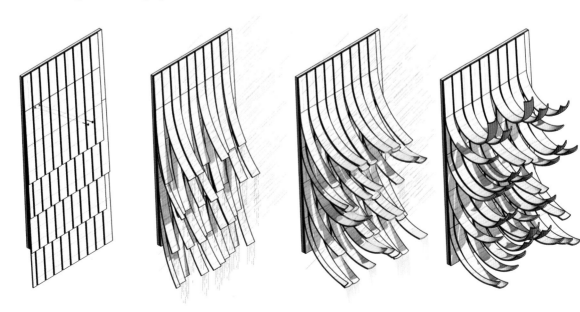

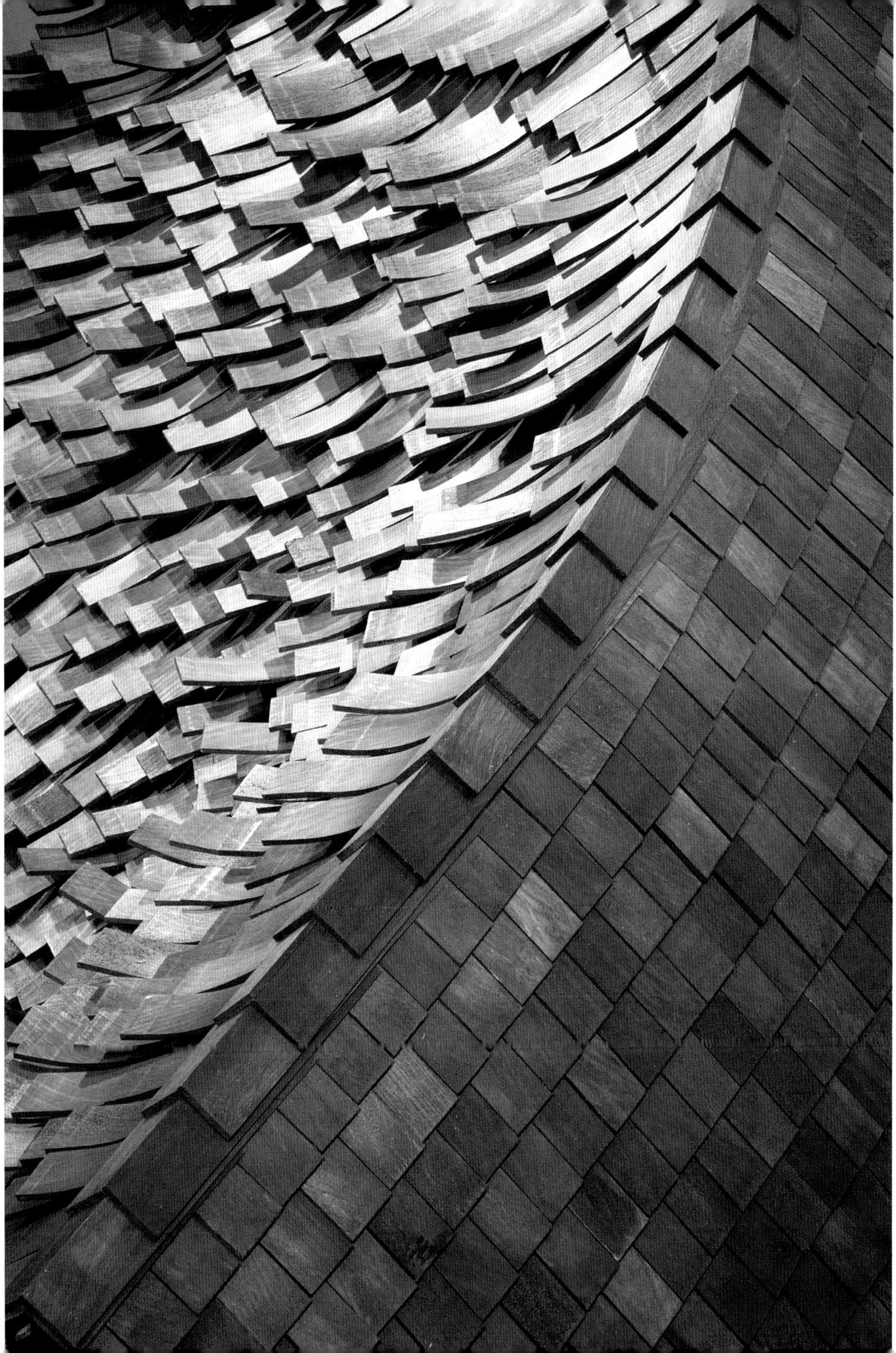

ZOOLOGICAL EIOSPHERE

ZOOLOGICAL BIOSPHERE

Designed by the Mediated Matter group at the Massachusetts Institute of Technology's Media Lab, the *Silk Pavilion* represents an entirely new approach to the use of biology in the design and construction of buildings. Here we see architects more carefully and deliberately studying the habits, behaviors, and patterns of animals, and then partnering with them, rather than merely emulating them. Architects are leveraging what swarms, herds, and schools of animals already do by actually including them in the process of material fabrication and helping them make decisions about the geometry in their work. This represents a new mode of control in the world of biologically inspired work.[1] Different from a method in which designers work intuitively, this method positions architects as strategists who opportunistically set carefully orchestrated systems into play without concern for the precise nature of their outcome. The animals call the shots. Architects can merely set the parameters, then step back and see how things unfold.

This is what Neri Oxman and the Mediated Matter group did with the *Silk Pavilion*. The project represents a radical departure from expectations of material use with a substance not conventionally employed in architecture. The pavilion utilizes the silk from silkworms—and more importantly, the natural process of silk production by the living caterpillars—for its construction (see pp 130–31). Oxman and her team first tracked the cocoon-building movements of silkworms and then created a panelized armature for the pavilion by programming a robotic arm to weave silk threads according to these movements. After sixty-five hundred live silkworms were placed on the fibrous scaffolding, they completed the structure with their own silk deposits.

The silkworms produced variation in the final surface as a result of their tendency to migrate to areas of darkness and density. With this knowledge, the team produced a pavilion structure that varied in density and in the amount of light it captured. The silkworms completed the work; they followed these patterns like a road map, depositing more silk where the designers wanted density and less where they wanted porosity. In the *Silk Pavilion*, insects contribute the inspiration, material, and subcontracting services to the project. This project, along with others reviewed in this chapter, represent the most seamless marriage to date between biology and design. In these types of projects architects must deeply understand the animals they are studying. To do so they must first collaborate with disciplines outside architecture, such as science, entomology, or zoology. They must be able to converse in the language of these disciplines, and they must be able to articulate the importance of their work to increasingly broad and diverse audiences. This is precisely what Oxman and her Mediated Matter group has managed to do. The effective communication of this work, which has been published in platforms outside architecture, seems to resonate with a broad audience and has established traction outside the small circles of architectural research.

Background

Since prehistoric times humanity has been deeply affected by the animal kingdom—and exerted a profound influence over it. Given our evolutionary proximity to animals and insects, as well as our identification with particular zoological species as having remarkable similarities to our own, it is no surprise that *Homo sapiens* have long studied the zoosphere in order to determine our most advantageous relationship with it—whether for our own benefit or for mutual gain. The designed environment has been deeply affected by animal husbandry practices, the exploitation of animate organisms for material resources or labor, the mimicry of animal morphologies and behaviors, and the blurring of animal life and human technology.

From a resource perspective, humans have utilized animals and insects for food, materials, and energy since before recorded history. Hunting is the principal method employed for this kind of use, which treats animals as sources of harvestable assets. Early humans developed the means to preserve animal skins to augment their own, whether as clothing or architectural cladding. Nomadic cultures and communities migrating to new climates made particular use of animal skins as protective coverings for their shelters. Fig. 1

Animal domestication, the development of a mutually beneficial relationship between animals and humans, deeply influenced the course of human civilization.[2] Domestication led to more predictable supplies of resources and transformed wild and often dangerous creatures into farm companions (e.g., wolves became

1. Eskimo natives in front of
hide-covered tents, East Cape
Village, Siberia, Russia, 1885

2. *Standing Glass Fish*, by Frank
Gehry, Walker Art Museum,
Minneapolis, Minnesota, 1986

dogs, wild boars became pigs). The incorporation of animals into the regular operations of early societies transformed land use and mobility—horseback riding, the plow, and the cart directly influenced the development of cities and transportation networks—as well as structured the land-based flows of material resources.

Over the course of millennia humans shaped the domesticated zoosphere by selective breeding, with the intent to elevate desirable traits while diminishing undesirable ones. This effort may be considered a grand multigenerational, multinational design project —insofar as the progressive manipulation of the genetic content and behavior of animals has produced creatures tailored to human desire, which would not have existed otherwise. This monumental endeavor intensified with industrialization, as animals became mass-produced commodities for widespread distribution—thus increasing the demand for large quantities of predictable products.

Humanity's effort to harvest animal resources has been accompanied by a profound interest in the nature of animal features, behaviors, and communal organizations. Early humans studied animals and their particular capabilities in order to increase their own means of survival, developing technologies to augment certain features—or compensate for their absence. Furs insulated naked bodies, for example, while spears and swords made up for the lack of horns or claws, and primitive shelters—the first

architecture—served as protective dens or nests. Later technological developments borrowed other animal capacities for human use—such as flight, audiovisual surveillance (e.g., radar, night vision), or aquatic mobility (e.g., wetsuits, scuba equipment). In this sense, technology might be seen as a way to extend human potential by neutralizing the advantages exhibited by other species. Architecture itself has also appropriated animal characteristics—be it thermal insulation or dynamic, operable assemblies.

In the history of architecture, the zoosphere has also been a powerful source of symbolism and metaphor. Fig. 2 From the komainu lions guarding Shinto shrine entrances to the granite gargoyles spouting rainwater from the roofs of Gothic churches, animal iconography has been an important repository for cultural meaning in architecture. The Big Duck, built in 1931 and later popularized by architect Robert Venturi as an example of architectural symbolism, has come to represent one of the most obvious— and uncritical—allegorical expressions in building. Other precedents highlight the representation of animal capacities, such as Ron Herron's Walking City proposal of 1964: an enormous mobile structure designed to roam freely in search of resources. Today, appearance and function have become intertwined, as architects are increasingly focused on the performative dimensions of animal physiognomy and behavior.

Silk Pavilion

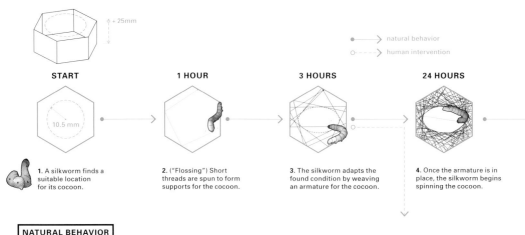

natural behavior
human intervention

START   **1 HOUR**   **3 HOURS**   **24 HOURS**

+ 25mm

10.5 mm

1. A silkworm finds a suitable location for its cocoon.

2. ("Flossing") Short threads are spun to form supports for the cocoon.

3. The silkworm adapts the found condition by weaving an armature for the cocoon.

4. Once the armature is in place, the silkworm begins spinning the cocoon.

NATURAL BEHAVIOR

MODIFIED BEHAVIOR

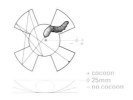

+ cocoon
25mm
– no cocoon

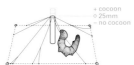

+ cocoon
25mm
– no cocoon

Research & Development
The team from M.I.T. and Tufts tested surface morphologies at varying heights. They found that a silkworm begins to build its cocoon in a space greater than 25 mm. It will then add threads to make an armature appropriate for the cocoon. When the available space is less than 25 mm, the silkworm's response is the same. Unable to achieve its goal, the silkworm gets caught in a kind of "do-while loop" of flossing. It will add threads of silk in a futile attempt to make a good space for building. This understanding created a data set of behaviors and production tendencies that allowed for a translation between animal behavior and design objectives.

Anchorage

6500 km

Houston

6,500 silkworms were used to produce the Silk Pavilion.

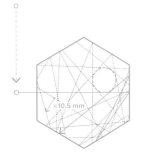

<10.5 mm

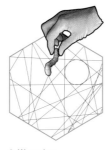

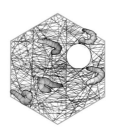

1. Feedback
A strategically programmed CNC tool wove an armature designed to keep the silkworm in the flossing stage.

2. Wranglers
Designers place the silkworm on the armature to begin working.

3. Flossing
Without the requisite space for a cocoon, the silkworms endlessly weave between the provided lines.

4. Fabrication
A biologically "printed" surface of silk.

Industrial harvest:
In commercial production, the cocoon is dropped in boiling water to terminate the animal and preserve the silk. The dead silkworm is eliminated and the thread is unwound.

21 DAYS

cocoon silk is spit

modified saliva dissolves silk

moth pushes through soft spot

26 HOURS   **50 HOURS**   **72 HOURS**

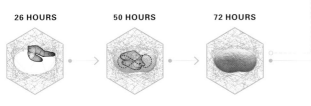

5. The silkworm weaves its cocoon with an unbroken thread up to 1.5 km long.

6. The silkworm weaves layers by rapidly moving its head in a figure-eight pattern (once every second).

7. The cocoon is made of many layers of sticky sericin-coated silk.

8. After approximately three weeks, a mature moth emerges from the cocoon and finds a mate. A female lays between 150 and 300 eggs.

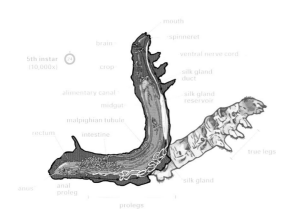

5th instar
(10,000x)   74

mouth

spinneret

brain

ventral nerve cord

crop

silk gland duct

alimentary canal

silk gland reservoir

midgut

malpighian tubule

intestine

rectum

true legs

anus

anal proleg

silk gland

prolegs

BOMBYX MORI
(mulberry silkworm)

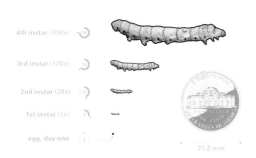

4th instar (700x)

3rd instar (120x)

2nd instar (20x)

1st instar (1x)

egg, day one

21.2 mm

24 DAYS

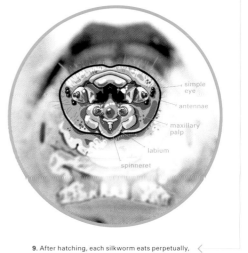

simple eye

antennae

maxillary palp

labium

spinneret

9. After hatching, each silkworm eats perpetually, stopping only to moult. The developed silkworm's anatomy, physiology, and behavior support the construction of a cocoon, allowing it to transition to its adult form.

Material Basis and Behaviors

A zoologically attuned architecture depends on an understanding of growth and form. Two foundational experts on these topics were D'Arcy Thompson and Alan Turing, who developed principles of *morphogenesis*.[3] Morphogenesis is the process by which animals take on their shape and appearance, over time, based on genetics (nature) and environment (nurture). Thompson and Turing explained that animal cell development results from differential growth in multiple directions, creating particular patterns of development. The contemporary study of this cell pattern development is known as evolutionary developmental (evo devo) biology.

Evo devo biology explains that all animals are made of the same genetic material, but that differences in final form emerge from a process by which those genes "turn on or off" at different times in an organism's growth.[4] This differential DNA firing results in a particular spatial distribution of cells during the embryonic development of an organism, giving rise to particular forms of tissues, organs, and overall body anatomy. Fig. 3 For example, in some of the birds that Charles Darwin studied on the Galapagos Islands,

The same genes are involved in making a sharp, pointy beak or a big, broad, nut-cracking beak. What makes all the difference is how much you turn a gene on, when you turn it on, when you turn it off—the subtle differences in regulation. Specific genes are essential to make any beak, but it's the tweaking—the amount of the gene, the timing of the gene, the duration of the gene—that's actually doing the trick.[5]

Architects and designers leverage knowledge of how organisms grow through several different working methods. For example, they might develop material fabrication strategies emulating growth patterns found in animals, resulting in material assemblies that more precisely accommodate shifting structural, programmatic, or environmental constraints. This strategy would represent, in evo devo terms, a genetic approach to building design—controlling material during its growth stage or while a building is under construction. As a second example, architects might

produce buildings that, rather than grow like biology, perform like biology after they are built (e.g., innovative student projects in which buildings breathe like a lung or insulate themselves in the manner of fur). This strategy would represent an epigenetic approach to building production—controlling material after its growth stage, or after a building is constructed. As a third, entirely different strategy, architects might leverage an understanding of the animal itself, often working hand in hand with biologists to predict behaviors and movement patterns to allow animals to actually participate in the construction of buildings.

Technology

Emerging zoosphere-focused technologies are based on the advanced study and utilization of animal and insect material resources, new approaches to emulating performance and behavior, and sophisticated bioengineering efforts that synthesize animal and synthetic media. Research activities concern either particular anatomical elements of animals, such as bones, muscles, or sensory organs, or physical constructions made by animals (animal architecture), such as webs, nests, shells, and so forth. In either case, both physical form and performance are subjects of intense scrutiny.

One of the distinguishing capacities of the zoosphere is mobility. The free movement of macroscopic-scaled creatures requires sophisticated, integrated systems of muscular and skeletal frameworks. Scientists continue to investigate the mechanics of mobility for robotics, prosthetics, shock absorption, and other applications involving moving, interlinked components.

4. Artificial Jellyfish,
by the Wyss Institute at
Harvard University

5. Shrilk, by the Wyss
Institute at Harvard
University

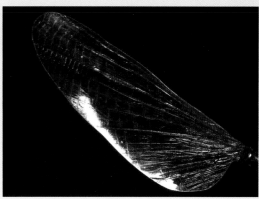

Two traditional manifestations of robotics—widgeto-phora, which consists of a cobbled-together assembly of components, and anthropoidea, which assumes anthropomorphic format—are now being supplanted by zoomorpha, a classification of robot based directly on particular animal species.[6] Researchers at the Sant'Anna School of Advanced Studies in Pisa, Italy, are building zoobots that emulate lampreys and octopus arms, for example.[7] These intelligent machines can navigate quickly through water, squeezing into tight spaces if necessary. They are made from interior springs of elastic nickel-titanium alloy wrapped in an outer casing of silicone with embedded pressure sensors. In another example, scientists at Harvard University and the California Institute of Technology developed a robotic jellyfish made from rat muscle tissue and flexible polymer film.[8] Fig. 4 When activated by electrodes, the biomechanical device propels itself through water like a medusa jellyfish. Other examples of zoomorpha include cyber clams, gecko lizards, shrews, and dragonflies. The proliferation of these small biomimetic devices suggests that architecture may also be a ripe territory for study. Buildings could make use of assemblies of self-regulating systems, for example, that control airflow, harness energy, treat waste, and self-heal when degraded.

From a material perspective, zoological substances such as chitin, bone, or skin are fertile territories for research and development. The Wyss Institute for Biologically Inspired Engineering at Harvard developed a material intended to mimic insect cuticle. The composite is called *shrilk* because of its constituent

proteins from silk and chitin—which is extracted from disposed shrimp shells.[9] Fig. 5 A potential future replacement for plastic, shrilk is stronger than aluminum, but only half the weight, and is completely biodegradable. As Kyoto University scientists have shown, chitin has also proved to be a potential candidate for light-transmitting displays once polymerized in a bath of acrylic resin.[10] Researchers have also been scrutinizing bone, creating synthetic materials that replicate natural functional gradient structures of hydroxyapatite mineral and collagen protein.[11]

Skin's multiple functions—such as protection, heat transfer, and regeneration—have motivated the development of new biomimetic technologies. Microfluidic glazing, for example, is a water-infused window system that reduces peaks in exterior surface temperature.[12] The liquid-cooled glass emulates the dilation of skin blood vessels that accelerate heat transfer to the surrounding air. Skin's regenerative capability is replicated in materials like self-repairing textiles, which are made from microcapsules of healing agent suspended in liquid polyurethane.[13] Other research efforts aim to replicate vibrant surface phenomena, such as the structural color of butterfly wings or ultrareflective fish scales of light-reflective guanine crystals.[14]

As described previously, the zoosphere represents a rich repository of multisensory capabilities offering the promise to extend our own sensory potential. A fascination with arthropods' multifaceted eyes has inspired scientists to create new light-directing films, solar collectors, and other advanced optical devices.

133

Zoological Biosphere

Researchers at the University of Illinois developed a camera that employs an array of microlenses with a structure similar to insect eyes.[15] The new synthetic eye, which integrates the tiny lens arrays with photodetectors and electronics, is also composed of flexible, rubbery materials to allow for lifelike stretching and deformation. Scientists have also sought to mimic the ultrasonic capacity of animal species like bats with technologies such as architectural echolocation, a tool that employs a computer algorithm to generate three-dimensional spatial maps using only auditory information.[16]

Not only are zoological materials and behaviors of technological interest, so are the substances and methods that animals and insects employ to shape their own environments. One of the most commonly studied precedents of animal architecture is the spider's web and its constituent material, dragline silk, which is known to be stronger than steel with a much lower embodied energy. In the late 1990s Nexia Biotechnologies developed BioSteel, an artificial spider silk that reportedly outperformed Kevlar in terms of strength and durability, and which was made from spider silk protein grown in transgenic goats' milk.[17] The Japanese company Spiber also created a synthetic spider thread using bioengineered bacteria and proteins extruded through a hollow, super-thin needle.[18] Other popular precedents of zoological construction include nacre, which inspired the creation of the clay nanosheet–based Plastic Steel, and mussel glue, which stimulated the development of a polymer composite that models the strong underwater adhesion of byssal holdfast fibers.[19]

Application

Architecture's relationship with the zoosphere offers rich potential as well as imminent challenges. The increased complexity, component interdependency, and continual transformation of the designed environment has encouraged the consideration of buildings as organisms rather than static, industrially produced objects. This paradigm is reinforced by the increased use of smart materials, dynamic systems, and robotics with both metaphorical and literal connections to the animal world. The following examples illustrate a partial spectrum of architecture's evolving relationship with the domain of animals and insects.

The utilization of animal-based resources has progressed from the direct use of bones and hides to the cultivation of ingredients for experimental and unexpected materials. Jack Munro's Blood Bricks, for example, are made of cow's blood collected from an abattoir, which is mixed with an anticoagulant and preservative, as well as sand.[20] To make the bricks the London-based architect studied historical African practices of mixing blood with plaster to create more durable building finishes. A related material is Qmilk, a textile created from milk.[21] While searching for a fabric alternative for allergy-prone clients, German microbiologist Anke Domaske developed a process that transforms the casein protein in milk into a biocompatible fabric. Similar in texture to silk, the quick-drying, hypoallergenic, antibacterial, and durable material requires much less energy, water, and human labor than the manufacture of other textiles. Because its fibers can embody different properties and textures, Qmilk is an open platform for future experimentation.

In addition to material resources, animal habitats continue to provide direction for contemporary architecture. Architect Andrew Kudless interrogates zoological constructions to create his own architectural assemblages of cells, folds, and chrysalises that are loosely based on various morphologies of animal and insect domains. "I am drawn to what might be called animal architectures, or the artifacts of nonhuman (and some even nonliving) builders," says Kudless. "The material is not living itself, but it has been constructed and left behind by more complex systems."[22] Large buildings have also become experimental territories for the adoption of environmental wisdom imbued within animal habitats. For example, Mick Pearce's Eastgate Centre in Harare, Zimbabwe, is a mixed-use commercial midrise building designed to emulate the displacement ventilation-based cooling effect found in termite mounds, thus requiring no air conditioning.[23]

The rapidly advancing field of robotics has profound implications for architecture. Mimicking the airborne construction practices of wasps and bees, Flight Assembled Architecture is a mobile robotics experiment developed by ETH Zürich professor Raffaello D'Andrea and architects Gramazio & Kohler.[24] Fig. 6 The first installation to be built by

flying machines, the project utilizes software-controlled flying robots to place foam bricks individually in order to construct a large open-weave structure. In a bizarre twist of another robotics project, North Carolina State University scientists employed live cockroaches as remote-controlled first responders to locate survivors in collapsed buildings.[25] The cyborg insects, wired with microcontrollers connected to their antennae and cerci, symbolize a new era of human-centered dominion.

The greatest concern now facing the zoosphere is a rapid loss of biodiversity, with 25 percent or more land-based species expected to disappear by 2050.[26] Climate change is the leading cause of this loss, although other pressures, such as increased development and resource depletion, pose additional challenges for the zoosphere. Building construction's significant role in these changes has motivated architects to take action and find ways to improve architecture's influence on, and relationship with, species other than our own. Recognition of the restricting effects of human development on wildlife migration has motivated the design of wildlife corridors that connect core reserves without interruption, providing critical access to expanded habitats and breeding grounds. The decline of important urban wildlife species has also inspired architects to design new habitats conducive for their survival. Elevator B, for example, is a structure designed especially for bees.[27] Fig. 7 At twenty-two feet (7 m) tall, the tower of steel, glass, and wood serves a colony of honeybees that were found in a nearby decaying grain mill. Described as an apartment building for the insects, Elevator B was a response to a competition held by the University of Buffalo's Ecological Practices Research Group, which asked for a living structure in which local bees could thrive within an urban environment and that would serve as an educational demonstration project. Given the worrisome decrease in bee populations, this project demonstrates one way in which architecture can be used as a tool for preserving biodiversity.

Chrysalis (III)

Paris, France, 2012
MATSYS

Chrysalis (III) by Andrew Kudless of MATSYS is an experimental wood veneer installation at the Centre Pompidou in Paris. It is motivated by the cellular, self-organizing behavior of sea barnacles, specifically their ability to pack themselves as densely as possible into an efficient pattern, despite their irregularity. The project simulates the complexity found in the barnacles through dynamic, parametric computer modeling. A digital animation of the project's hexagonal modules relaxing into their final configuration reveals the compelling process, akin to soap bubbles moving and adjusting to one another in a sink full of dirty dishes.

Similar packing projects have encountered difficult fabrication challenges. The innovation in *Chrysalis (III)* lies at the vertices of its cells, which are allowed to float and move along a curved surface. Their connected edges are designed to act like flexible springs. As they adjust dynamically to fluctuate in the overall shape of their substrate, or to varying sizes of their neighbors, their individual components maintain an order and logic that renders them easily constructible. In other words, they can always be unfolded flat and cut out of sheet material with a laser cutter, no matter their width, depth, or orientation. The project learns, from its barnacle precedent, how to grow visual complexity out of a simple set of rule-constrained behaviors. This informs both its appearance and the surprisingly simple logic of its fabrication and construction.

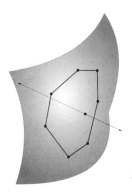 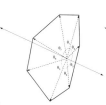  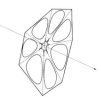

1. Find the surface normal of the cell edge centroid

2. Create vectors from centroid to cell edge vertices and find the angle sum

3. Iteratively move the centroid along the normal vector until the angle sum equals 360°

4. Create surfaces and holes and then join into a polysurface

5. Unfold the polysurface and prepare for fabrication

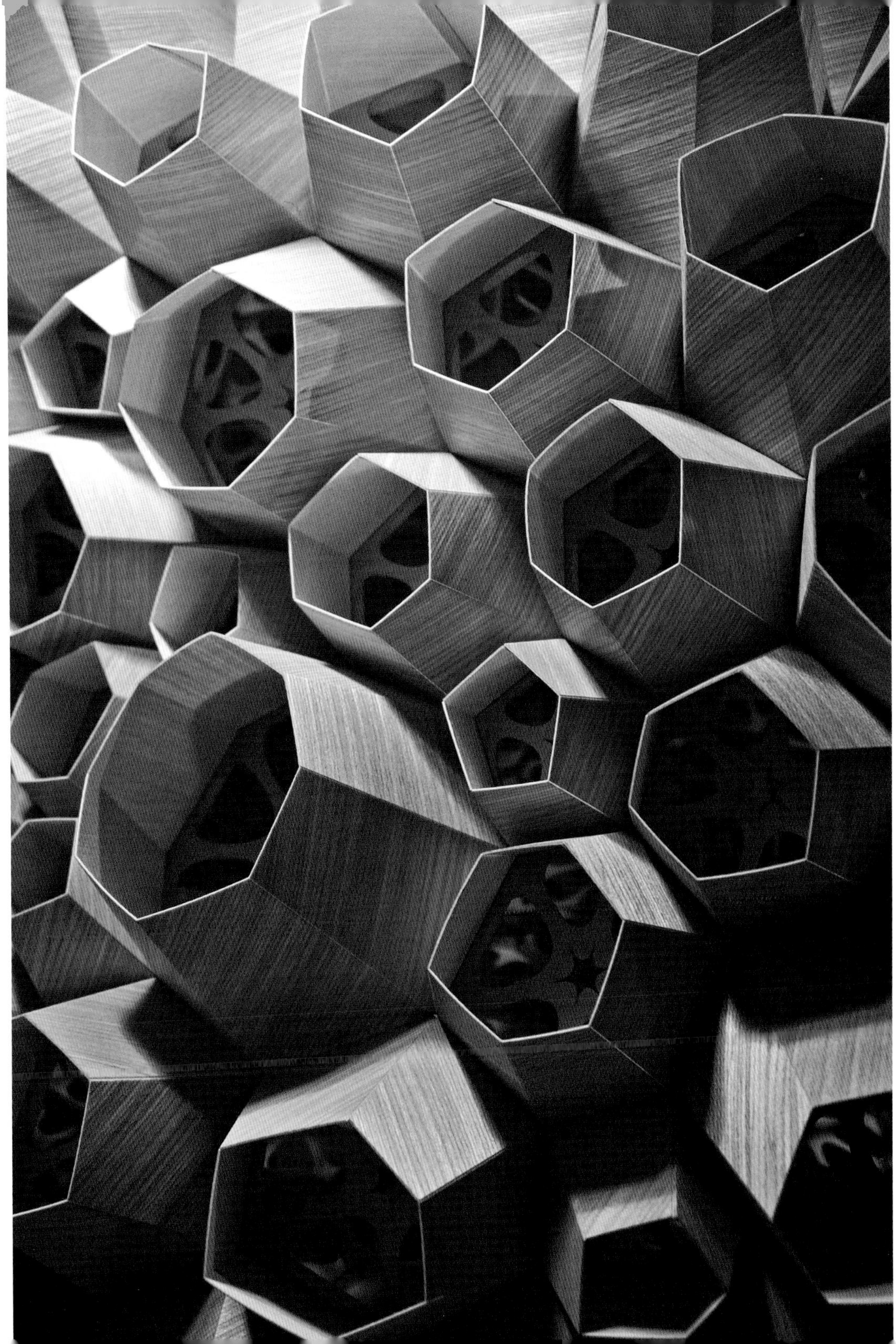

Homeostatic Facade

New York, New York (Prototype), 2011
Decker Yeadon

Decker Yeadon's Homeostatic Facade represents the transliteration of a primary anatomical function of animals to buildings. The biomimetic prototype, which is powered by artificial muscles, is an advanced solar control system for building envelopes. As such, it employs the operations of animal musculature to regulate daylight penetration.

The Homeostatic Facade uses dielectric elastomers (DE), which are a type of electroactive polymer (EAP) that undergo large strains with the introduction of electrical current. Decker Yeadon developed an actuator made of a pliable plastic substrate sheathed in DE, which in turn is clad in silver electrodes. When electricity is provided to the electrodes, they distribute the charge evenly across the elastomer, causing it to expand. This expansion then forces the polymer core to flex. The designers provided a roller at the top edge of the core to ensure fluid movement of the elastomer.

In operation the Homeostatic Facade is a maze-like network of flexing musculature in which similarly spaced ribbons of curvilinear DE surfaces elongate and contract, adjusting the degree of solar shading as needed. In this way the system provides maximum opacity during the times of most intense direct solar exposure, and minimum obstruction when solar heat gain is not a concern. The outer silver electrodes enhance light-delivery, reflecting exterior radiance when open and interior illumination when closed. Because of the facade's distributed configuration, sunlight regulation may be highly localized—unlike other shading mechanisms that treat solar control uniformly. This adaptable focus, coupled with the fact that DE consume relatively little energy, results in a low-power approach to active solar control.

In the broader context of operable building envelopes, the Homeostatic Facade constitutes a shift away from early electromechanical facade systems and their aggregations of discrete motorized parts. In the spirit of its model biology, it takes advantage of a response mechanism inherent in the material itself—one that requires significantly less energy or manual intervention than its predecessors.

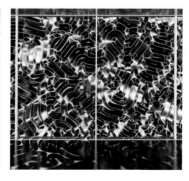

▲ Interior elevation phases

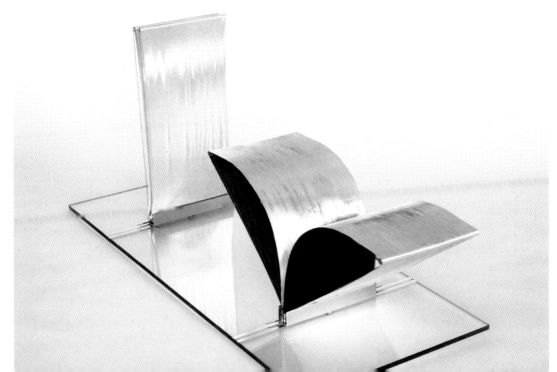

▸ Dielectric elastomer (DE) demonstration model

Zoological Biosphere

ICD/ITKE Research Pavilion

Stuttgart, Germany, 2012
Achim Menges and Jan Knippers

In November 2012 the Institute for Computational Design (ICD) and the Institute of Building Structures and Structural Design (ITKE) at the University of Stuttgart, led by professors Achim Menges and Jan Knippers, completed the fabrication and installation of a unique fiber-woven pavilion. Strikingly beautiful from a distance, the pavilion's true innovation comes into focus through the examination of its digitally woven skin. The pavilion stands at about ten feet tall (3 m) and twenty-four feet (7 m) in diameter, yet it weighs only seven hundred pounds (320 kilograms) and measures just over one-eighth inch (3 mm) thick. It is the product of ongoing research collaboration between architects, engineers, biologists, and students. As a precedent, the team examined lobster exoskeletons, specifically focusing on material differentiation along the cross section of the organism's shell. Variation in stresses placed on the shell causes its microscopic fibers to migrate from parallel to perpendicular orientation. In the pavilion, similar changes in fiber orientation efficiently accommodate the flow of forces through the structure. The resulting pattern of layered strands in the shell forms a visual map of those forces flowing through its surface.

The research team relied on a six-axis robotic arm to accurately weave the resin-saturated carbon and glass fibers together. A temporary steel frame formed an armature across which fibers were being woven. To protect it from the weather, the frame sat on a rotating platform in a provisional structure near the site of the pavilion. As the frame rotated slowly on its turntable, the robotic arm went to work laying down some twenty miles of fiber. Successive layers of fiber strands are clearly visible in the resulting translucent material assembly. Once the fabrication of the pavilion was completed, its steel frame was removed and it was carried to its final resting place, not with heavy cranes or lifts but with a small group of students who each supported one of its legs.

The ICD/ITKE Research Pavilion's diaphanous skin owes its remarkable strength to the shockingly thin shell structures of Spanish architect Félix Candela. The project successfully merges unique modes of computation and material design with robotic fabrication and biomimetics to present new ways to consider lightweight, materially efficient architectural structures. It offers innovative ways to consider the use of fibrous, woven material in building construction.

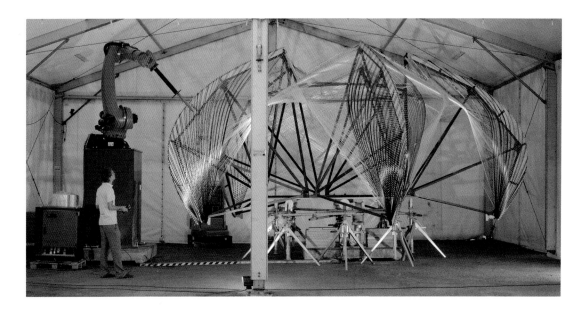

One Ocean Pavilion

Yeosu, South Korea, 2012
SOMA and Knippers Helbig
Advanced Engineering

One Ocean Pavilion exemplifies the attempt to translate zoological performance into architecture. Designed by SOMA architects with Knippers Helbig Advanced Engineering, the pavilion was the winning competition entry for the Theme Pavilion of the World Expo 2012 in Yeosu, South Korea. Based on the expo's conceptual focus on sustainable coastal development—with the advertised theme of "the living ocean and coast"—the project team proposed a waterfront building with a prominent design feature resembling gills, the anatomical organ that supplies oxygen to fish.[28]

The inland facade of One Ocean is composed of 108 vertical lamellas, which open and close based on changing solar conditions or programmed choreography. The lamellas are made of glass fiber–reinforced polymer (GFRP) of heights ranging from 10 to 43 feet (3 to 13 m) and are designed with low bending stiffness and high tensile strength in order to accommodate repeated elastic deformations. Developed from a research project on the scalability of biological mechanisms to architecture that was conducted at the ITKE, the lamellas demonstrate a dynamic material process, rather than an industrial-style mechanical approach.

Actuators located at the top and bottom of the GFRP strips control movement by exerting compression forces via servomotor-driven screw spindles. This two-sided constriction causes elastic deformation in the lamellas, in the form of lateral rotation, thus opening the facade to reveal interior glazing. Solar panels on the pavilion roof provide energy to the actuators, which are synchronized by a computer-driven bus system that allows for optional control over individual elements. Because the paired actuators frequently work in opposition to each other, the system is designed to recapture the residual power generated for enhanced energy efficiency.

The lamellas that cover the 460-foot-long (140 m) facade most closely resemble the operations of the operculum—the protective outer skin flap that allows the flow of water to the gills of fish. Although the dynamic cladding system regulates light and view rather than oxygen, the translation of a biological operation into an adaptive material capacity represents this project's most significant contribution to the advancement of responsive architecture.

The Truffle

Costa da Morte, Spain, 2010
Ensamble Studio

The Truffle (*La Trufa*) is a study in the ritualization of metabolic processes in architecture. Designed by Ensamble Studio, the Truffle is a small beach house on the Atlantic coastline in northwest Spain. The architects conceived the structure as an inhabitable stone that emerges from the ground, and developed a carefully choreographed sequence of construction procedures that are as compelling as the end result.

The architects first dug a hole in the raw earth, piling excess dirt around the perimeter. After pouring a concrete slab, they stacked hay bales to create a compressible organic formwork in the center of the slab. The architects then poured successive layers of concrete in the interstitial spaces between earth and hay, piling up more dirt and hay bales until reaching the top, which they covered with a final layer of concrete. Once the concrete cured, the architects removed the earth and carved out apertures using stonecutting machines.

At this stage Ensamble Studio employed a young calf named Paulina to eat the compressed hay occupying the interior of the Truffle. After one year Paulina digested the entire 1,700 cubic feet (50 cu. m) of hay, finally revealing the inhabitable interior of the Truffle—and growing into a full-sized cow weighing over 600 pounds (300 kilograms) in the process. Thus, not only did Paulina ingest all the building's internal formwork—the formwork was also transformed into an adult cow, insofar as she metabolized this excess building material in order to grow to a mature size. The residue, or the material uncovered from the earth and not devoured by Paulina, is now the architecture.[29]

The patient, ceremonial nature of the Truffle's construction—and in particular the animal-based digestive process—represents a significant and highly unexpected approach to building. Typically formwork is treated as a waste material, rather than food. In this case the intentional integration of a zoological metabolic cycle in building creates a symbiotic interchange and results in a notably improved ecological outcome over conventional methods.

NOOSPHERE

"This Will Kill That" is a chapter from Victor Hugo's *The Hunchback of Notre Dame* that continues to haunt architects.[1] In the essay Hugo presages the replacement of the building with the book as the primary didactic physical medium. Since the development of the printing press, the building has been relieved of its responsibility to impart knowledge to society, which has since been assumed by the versatility of the printed page. The Korean Pavilion at the Shanghai Expo reimagines the role of the building as a teaching medium by integrating architectural form and the form of language (see pp 150–51). Designed by Mass Studies, the structure is a three-dimensional interpretation of the modern Korean *Hangul* alphabet in scales ranging from inches to multistory volumes. Two types of cladding—white laser-cut steel composite panels and painted aluminum panels—define the exterior and interior facades, respectively. Although the alphabet characters are arranged in abstract geometric patterns, the building communicates a story—as the architects describe it: "Signs become spaces, and simultaneously, spaces become signs."[2]

There is universality to the Hangul alphabet. Its primary geometries are common to a number of cultures outside Korea, so everyone experiences the text on its walls through varying degrees of interpretation. This democratizing aspect of the project is common to much of the work presented in this chapter on the *noosphere*—the domain of human thought. Many architects are interested in using architecture as a medium for translation, offering translation and abstraction as a method for sharing information and engendering an atmosphere of community.

However, the materials of the Korean Pavilion cladding do more than simply communicate static words and phrases. Similar to the Skin project by P-06 Atelier, the negative spaces formed between the letters interact with natural and artificial light in particular, curated ways. Light and shadows produced by the words project different atmospheres in the daytime and nighttime. Sequential lighting installed behind the Hangul pixels, for example, highlights select letters on the exterior facade, producing what the architects refer to as text messages at large and small scales.[3] These messages are programmed to change from day to day; the building serves as a giant word search, revealing particular messages that are meaningful to the Expo visitors.

The Korean Pavilion is a wonderfully playful essay on the language of space and the space of language. It demonstrates the extent to which verbal and visual literacy are interconnected, leveraging language as a vehicle for the production of a new kind of dynamic architectural ornament. It enables architecture itself to communicate in previously unrealized ways, to produce a new kind of language, like that of social media or computer language, that are uniquely specific to the medium.

Background

Architecture developed not as an isolated discipline but as a field related directly to other human endeavors. According to Hugo, architecture emerged in parallel with human thought and language: "It was first an alphabet. A stone was planted upright to be a letter and each letter became a hieroglyph. And on every hieroglyph there rested a group of ideas, like the capital of a column. Thus primitive races of the same period 'wrote' all over the world."[4] Fig. 1 Architecture's basis in ideas, rather than mere substance, is one of its defining characteristics. Like language, architecture has evolved over time, becoming increasingly sophisticated and agile in order to embody more complex concepts. As the dissemination of knowledge has become more accessible and fluid over time, the methodologies and products of architecture have become increasingly enriched by information.

As described above, the noosphere refers to the sphere of human thought. Based on the Greek term *nous*, or mind, the noosphere is a concept developed by philosopher Édouard Le Roy, geochemist Vladimir Vernadsky, and philosopher Pierre Teilhard de Chardin, who proposed it as the evolutionary successor to the geosphere and biosphere.[5] According to historian Georgy Levit, Vernadsky believed that "human thought appears in the noosphere as a lawful manifestation of biospheric evolution, which can only be separated from it in abstraction."[6] This chapter considers the noosphere from Vernadsky's point of view, as an extension of the biosphere—and therefore endowed with its own natural principles, structures, and processes. This section also examines the related concepts of *technosphere* and *anthroposphere*, which concern the realms of human technology and human-modified environment.

Manuel De Landa uses material metaphors to describe the evolution of language in societies, stating that "social processes provide the 'cement' that hardens these deposits of linguistic sediment into more or less stable and structured entities."[7] Many schools of historical linguistics consider the development of communication to follow patterns similar to biological evolution. For example, isolation is a key factor in both language and biological development: "Much as reproductive isolation consolidates loose accumulations of genes into a new animal or plant species, communicative isolation transforms accumulations of linguistic replicators into separate entities."[8] Other factors such as mutation, natural selection, adaptation, and extinction may also be considered shared features.

In the history of architecture, the evolution of communication is evident in both the shared chronicles of building construction methods (information for building) as well as in the use of buildings as communications platforms (information in building). The former traces an arc from Vitruvius's *De Architectura* to the contemporary constellation of construction specifications, trade association guidelines, and practice-based research. The latter articulates a trajectory from early didactic buildings, such as the Karnak Temple Complex (3200 BCE) or Palace of Minos (1900 BCE), to today's multimedia-infused structures. Both have been dramatically influenced by significant developments in communication technologies, such as the printing press or the computer.[9]

Today, architecture increasingly navigates the interface between materiality and information. On the one hand, buildings are corporeal, but on the other, they are ephemeral, serving as repositories for ideas. Ultimately, the two merge in human consciousness. "A designer creates an architecture of information within the mind of the recipient of his work. Its structure is comprised of the stimuli that enter through assorted sensory perception channels. The stimuli, which are brought forth by the senses…are set up in the brain of the recipient and there emerges what we call 'an image.'"[10] Fig. 2 This image is laden with meaning, from behavioral cues to cultural symbolism, which builds on a viewer's past experiences in the construction of new ideas.

Material Basis and Behaviors

In his seminal book *A Thousand Years of Nonlinear History*, De Landa says: "Our languages may also be seen over time as momentary slowing downs or thickenings in a flow of norms that gives rise to a multitude of different structures."[11] He goes on to explain that our bodies, as humans, are only partially composed of flesh and bones, that there are whole other strata to what he refers to as the "BwO," or "body without organs." These strata include the sun, the earth's lava, the atmosphere, the hydrosphere, our genetic code, and finally our languages. Each strata exerts a force on the flow of biological life on the planet. And so it is only natural that we consider the nonorganic life of language, alongside the hydrosphere, atmosphere,

Korean Pavilion

"h"
"a"
"g,k"
"n"
"eu"
"r,l"
syllable 1   syllable 2

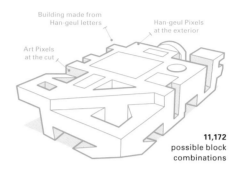

Building made from
Han-geul letters

Han-geul Pixels
at the exterior

Art Pixels
at the cut

11,172
possible block
combinations

Han-Geul

Han meant "great" in
archaic Korean and means
"Korean" in Sino-Korean.
Geul is the native
Korean word for "script."

2-5
Each block contains 2 to 5
letters. One must be a
consonant and one must
be a vowel.

24
Consonant and vowel
sounds are grouped
into blocks

Symbol as sound

Written Korean carries clues about its phonological
qualities. Each stroke in this *featural alphabet*
indicates specific characteristics about the sound
produced when a letter is read, including the place
and manner of articulation. This codification is
deployed consistently and was designed to make
the language easier to learn and understand. Some
examples and groupings are indicated below.
It is a convergence of behavior and representational
graphic. The English letters are an approximation
of the sounds produced by a native Korean speaker.

SAGITTAL SECTIONS

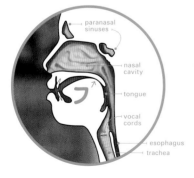

paranasal
sinuses

nasal
cavity

tongue

vocal
cords

esophagus

trachea

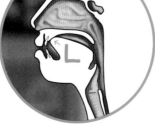

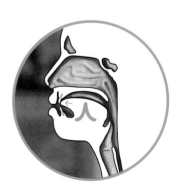

VELAR

"g"   "k"   "kk"

ALVEOLAR

"n"   "d"   "t"   "r,l"   "tt"

DENTAL

"s"   "j"   "ch"   "ss"   "jj"

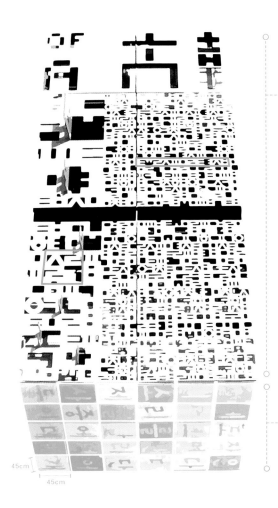

Sign as space

Unrelated language systems converge in the facade. Universal graphic forms and geometries are used in many written languages (see below). This creates a kind of "open source" graphic that creates opportunities for happenstantial readings throughout the architecture.

The "Han-Guel Pixels" are white digitally cut metal panels. The figure of each letter form is emphasized. Four different panel sizes are used to mark the exterior of the building. Light, shadow, and the location of the occupant affects the read.

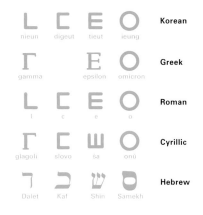

L	ㄷ	E	O	**Korean**
nieun	digeut	tieut	ieung	
Γ		E	O	**Greek**
gamma		epsilon	omicron	
L	ㄷ	E	O	**Roman**
l	c	e	o	
Γ	ㄷ	Ш	O	**Cyrillic**
glagoli	slovo	sa	onŭ	
ד	כ	שׁ	ם	**Hebrew**
Dalet	Kaf	Shin	Samekh	

Space as sign

Tens of thousands of tiles were both collected and created by renowned artist Ik-Joong Kang. These tiles offer another form of convergence. The "Art Pixels" are 45 × 45 cm. Each signed tile carries a simple message. All were sold after the Expo. The artist saw this as a way to recycle the building and to distribute the memory of a shared experience across the planet.

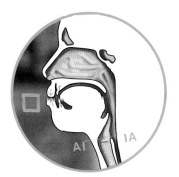

45cm

45cm

TRANSVERSE SUPERIOR SECTION A–A

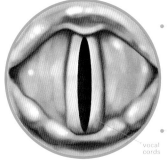

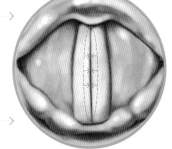

vocal cords

BILABIAL

"m"   "b"   "p"   "pp"

GLOTTAL FRICATIVE

"h"

GLOTTAL STOP

obsolete

and geosphere, as participating in the biological history of our planet and as occupying its own biological sphere, with all the attributes we associate with textbook definitions of life.

Lewis Thomas further emphasized the biological nature of language in his essay "Living Language," where he says "language is simply alive, like an organism…Words are the cells of language, moving the great body, on legs. Language grows and evolves, leaving fossils behind. The individual words are like different species of animals. Mutations occur. Words fuse, and then mate. Hybrid words and wild varieties or compound words are the progeny."[12] So, if, by De Landa's and Thomas's definitions, language is biological, what is its material foundation? To design around or with the material of language, on what must designers focus their research? To answer these questions, we might begin with the basic definition of language. The dictionary says language is "a method of human communication, either spoken or written, consisting of the use of words in a structured and conventional way."[13] Fig. 3 In computation, however, language is "a system of symbols and rules for writing programs or algorithms."[14] Less conventional definitions link it to behavior and thought. French linguist Ferdinand de Saussure observed, "a language can be compared to a sheet of paper. Thought is one side of the sheet and sound the reverse side. Just as it is impossible to take a pair of scissors and cut one side of the paper without at the same time cutting the other, so it is impossible in a language to isolate sound from thought, or thought from sound."[15]

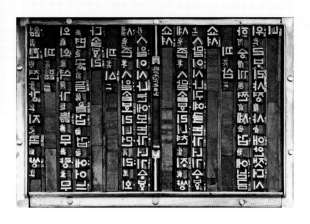

We quickly observe that language is not so easy to define. It consists of much more than the words we speak or the symbols we write. Rather, it shapes our thought and behavior; it is an artifact of our actions, a tracing of how our flesh and bone bodies (bodies *with* organs) behave and operate. As we zoom farther out, we observe that language has structure and hierarchy, that languages layer on one another in misaligned relationships that periodically find commonality at nodal points. It is at these nodal points that translation occurs: information is transferred from one network to another. Data transfer, then, is the entry point for architects to develop language into built form.

Technology

Just as humankind has exerted a growing influence on the planet, the impact of the noosphere has similarly increased because of the growing human population, the burgeoning archive of shared knowledge and creative production, and the advancement of communications technologies. Economist Julian Simon has declared the human mind to be "the ultimate resource," and writer Kevin Kelly credits humanity's progress with our shared, structured knowledge of science and technology, stating that "science is a collective action, and the emergent intelligence of shared knowledge is often superior to even a million individuals."[16] The technologies we have created from this shared knowledge have multiplied rapidly, and our global communications network—with its 170 quadrillion computer chips, 3 billion synthetic eyes, and consumption of 5 percent of the world's electricity —now exhibits a complexity similar to that of the human brain.[17] Thus the noosphere that spawned human tools has given rise to a technosphere that parallels the biological basis of human thought.

As technology advances, it continues to extend human sensory capabilities with the aim of making the invisible visible and the unknown known. New products and systems exhibit ever more lifelike capabilities of tracking, diagnosis, response, interaction, self-assembly, and self-replication with significant ramifications for architecture. For example, the Living City system is a platform that enables buildings to talk to one another.[18] Created by David Benjamin and Soo-in Yang, Living City consists of a network of small facade modules that collect data, exchange

4. SyNAPSE
project, by IBM
Research

5. BioTac,
by SynTouch
LLC

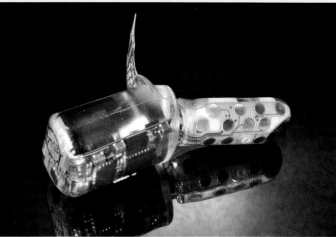

information with other buildings, compare the data, and communicate any needed changes (e.g., facade porosity, media display). KieranTimberlake architects have developed their own real-time climate data collection system, which boasts unprecedented resolution and responsiveness—allowing architects to incorporate immediate environmental feedback into the building design process.[19] Concern for the damaging effects of natural disasters and degradation via aging has motivated engineers from a number of institutions to develop sensor-based monitoring systems that track the physical health of infrastructure. These include both wired and wireless systems, as well as self-healing materials capable of making immediate local repairs. Human traffic is also increasingly monitored: Massachusetts Institute of Technology scientists have developed "Wi-Vi" (Wireless Vision), a technology that senses the presence and movements of people in buildings—through walls, closed doors, and other opaque building surfaces.[20] Although this tool may offer lifesaving capabilities during emergencies, it also raises concerns related to the growing loss of personal privacy. Regardless of its use, it presages a phenomenon that writer Bruce Sterling dubbed *spime*—the spatiotemporal tracking of any entity throughout its lifetime (and beyond).[21]

Emerging noospheric technologies also include approaches that replicate human anatomical processes in designed objects and assemblies. For example,

IBM's SyNAPSE project (Systems of Neuromorphic Adaptive Plastic Scalable Electronics) takes inspiration from the physical structure and performance of the human brain in order to create *neurosynaptic* computer chips that can rewire themselves based on different environmental stimuli.[22] Fig. 4 Stanford University researchers have developed an elastic sensor made of carbon nanotubes that is transparent and stretchable.[23] Called *super skin*, the flexible sensor may be stretched to over two times its original size without deformation and can detect a wide variety of pressures. A technology called BioTac developed by SynTouch LLC incorporates pressure and temperature sensors within a durable, deformable casing.[24] Fig. 5 Designed to function as a synthetic fingertip for robots as well as human prostheses, BioTac is made of a rigid sensor-filled core surrounded by a conductive fluid encased in an elastomeric material. Like human skin, BioTac can perceive minute changes in the immediate environment, which are communicated via embedded electrodes. Other anthropomimetic technologies have been applied directly to architecture: the Institute for Chemical and Bioengineering at ETH Zurich has developed a thermoresponsive polymer for building facades that emulates the function of human sweat glands.[25] Like our skin, it improves temperature regulation by releasing water above a set temperature—thus inducing a cooling response. As these examples—and the entire field of

Noosphere

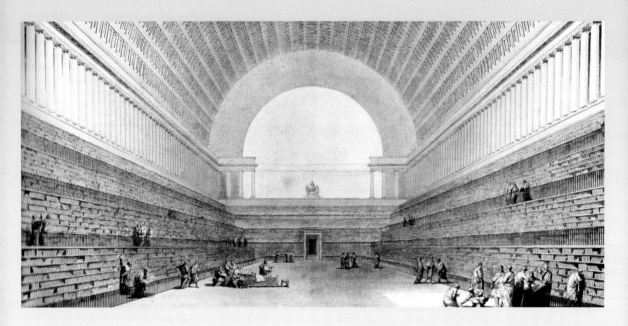

robotics—demonstrate, the designed environment will increasingly exhibit anthropomimetic behaviors and will be as much a mirror of human anatomical processes as it is a reflection of our intellectual aspirations.

Application

As posited earlier, language and thought are the material foundations of noosphere architecture. Rooting architecture in the immateriality of these topics results in vastly different interpretations and wildly unique experiments, extending the possibilities of how our built environments might participate in communication. There is a bigger leap here than in previous biological spheres, since the word *language* can be interpreted in so many different ways. While certainly the world has seen an explosion of digital displays, "jumbotrons," and projection surfaces in contemporary architecture, video technology is not the focus here. Rather, this work folds language, thought, and culture into its very infrastructure to pose larger questions about human discourse and its relevance to architectural production.

Some of the work advances how information is shared and distributed, rendering it democratically accessible. An early example of this is the eighteenth-century Bibliothèque Nationale, by Étienne-Louis Boullée. Fig. 6 Proposed as an addition to the French National Library in 1785, Boullée's scheme suggested that, for the first time, the state would take responsibility for collecting, ordering, and disseminating information for its citizens.[26] Previously, books were bound and chained, hidden away from the public, with limited access. The Bibliothèque Nationale project was radical at the time because it suggested an open arrangement of stacks where books were publicly displayed and easy to browse. Visitors would be free to explore the stacks and converse in the open about relevant, contemporary topics. Operating under a similar premise, Datagrove, by Future Cities Lab, collects and disseminates streaming social media through light and sound in an open public space in an effort to democratize data and information.

Other work incorporates communication into its very form, structure, or texture. Such is the case with Thomas Heatherwick's Seed Cathedral for the Shanghai Expo in 2010. Fig. 7 Designed to display some 250,000 seeds collected from the Kew Gardens' Millennium Seed Bank, the project is composed of 60,000 rods of clear acrylic, each 25 feet (7.5 m) long,

which protrude from the walls of the pavilion and
cantilever out into the air. These rods allow light to
infiltrate the interior space of the pavilion and serve
to backlight the seeds, which are cast into their thick
ends. The interior of the pavilion is like a giant,
analog display monitor that has been exploded into
thousands of tiny screens. Visitors not only learn
about local plant species but are also attuned to the
daily movement of the sun and to passing clouds and
birds in the sky. Since light is directed straight out
from the ends of the tubes, it seems to move with the
occupants, like a tracking spotlight that requires no
programming or electronics. In the Seed Cathedral
the system for communicating language also provides
light, cladding, material pattern, and tactility. Further,
that same system physically stores knowledge of the
biological world as seeds where each rod is like an
encapsulated word, idea, or data set. It is a building
where information is concretized and translated to a
material assembly of visual delight.

The projects that follow similarly wrestle with the
materiality of language, thought, and culture. While
vastly different, they have in common this shared
interest in architecture as a medium for communication. Some achieve this through decidedly analog,
material-intensive strategies, while others embrace
access to increasingly affordable technology to produce dynamic atmospheres informed by data flows. In
any case it is clear that these architects consider our
noosphere to be as legitimately biological as all the
more conventional natural spheres presented thus far.

Datagrove

San Jose, California, 2012
Future Cities Lab

Beyond the spoken word, there are many different forms of language, and even now, variations emerge in unexpected places. Take, for example, the new lexicon birthed by social media. In an article on the blog *Wordability*, Hugh Westbrook writes that one "interesting aspect of Twitter language is that it is conversational English, but expressed in written form, possibly leading to a new type of communication." [27] The content generated by this "new type of communication" is massive and somewhat divisive. No one could ever hope to comprehend it in all its permutations, nor could anyone comprehensively manage its vastness. But there it is, consistent and always present.

This data omniscience is what Future Cities Lab exploits in its *Datagrove* project. This public art project "listens" to the streams of data emerging from Twitter and represents it as a wall of pulsing light and sound. The project thrives on information. It renders both environmental, atmospheric data and social media into variably intensive projections. Sited in a public space in downtown San Jose, California, *Datagrove* provides a resting place where visitors can enjoy a choreography of subtle pulsations originating from sources near and far. The architects say of their project: "The grove's luminescent fibers gently sway with the breeze and respond to the proximity of visitors with quiet whispering sonic undulations." [28]

Datagrove universalizes the new language of Twitter and other social media. Writer Angelo Suico says in an article titled "Does 'Rick Rolling' Ring a Bell?" that "Internet lingo is something that constantly grows and evolves, and only the most dedicated Internet users are the most fit to keep up. This causes a cultural divide between different groups." [29] *Datagrove* ingests this new language and translates it, through the universal media of space, vision, sound, and light, into a meditative, democratic public space.

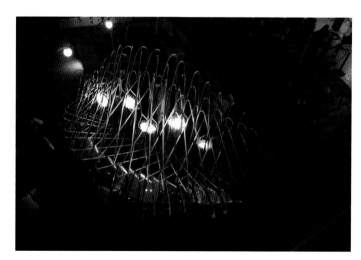

▲ Detail of custom electronic module

Dream Cube

Shanghai, China, 2010
Atelier Feichang Jianzhu (FCJZ)

The winning competition entry for the Centre Pompidou in 1971, by Renzo Piano and Richard Rogers, astounded the art world. When completed in 1977 the new museum in Paris's Beaubourg district appeared to be a machine turned inside out: rather than hide its contents behind a conventional facade, the building exposed its internal operations via an open framework of suspended mechanical and circulatory systems. Seeking to create "a flexible container and dynamic communications machine," the architects aimed to transform the museum typology into a new kind of technology-infused media platform.[30]

More than three decades later Atelier FCJZ architects sought to reinterpret Piano and Rogers's approach in their design for the Shanghai Corporate Pavilion at the 2010 World Expo. Making the case that building systems have become much more advanced and complex after thirty years of development, the designers pursued their own strategy to reveal the inner workings of the technology-themed pavilion and its underlying structure. Since the program called for environmentally focused design approaches, the architects utilized solar energy and water-harvesting infrastructure. They also incorporated repurposed waste material as a primary architectural feature, creating a dense matrix of transparent polycarbonate tubes made from recycled compact discs. They

infused this delicate three-dimensional lattice with a network of solar-powered LEDs and a rainwater-based mist system, transforming the pavilion into a resource-aware media vehicle for light and water displays.

Like the Centre Pompidou, the Dream Cube is an inhabitable mechanical tableau that lays bare its internal operations, visually communicating important sociotechnological aspirations of its time. In the Shanghai pavilion the architects' careful attention to resources allows visitors to experience the building not as a fixed entity but as an inhabitable conduit of material and energy flows. Demonstrating that creative conservation can be a principal ambition of technological enterprise, the Dream Cube represents a new chapter in human industry.

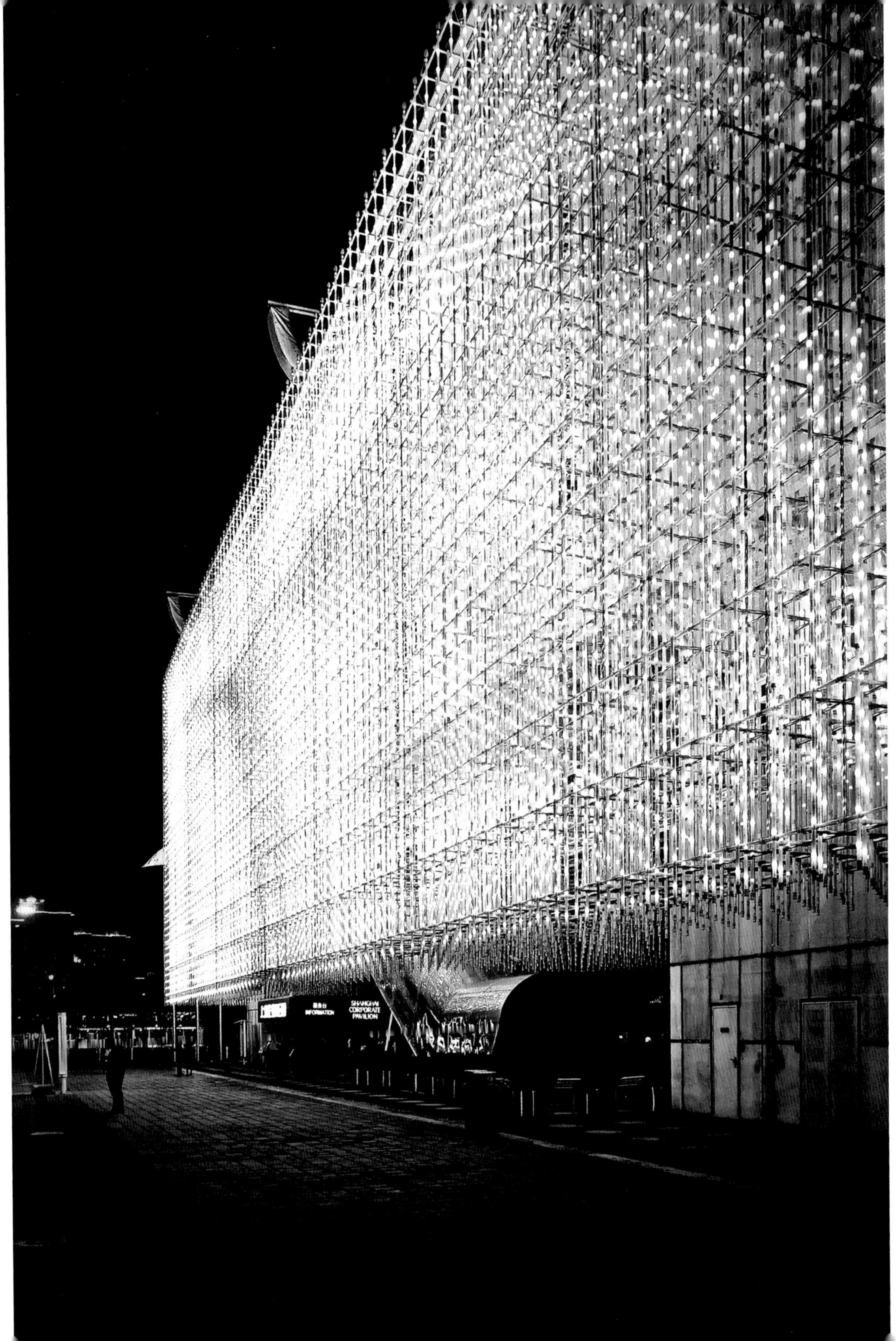
INFORMATION
SHANGHAI
CORPORATE
PAVILION

Hyper-Matrix

Yeosu, South Korea, 2012
Jonpasang

According to Victor Hugo, "The first records were simply squares of rock"—primitive building blocks that defined the elemental alphabet of architecture.[31] Although the connection between language and building is often abstract, a clear union is made in Hyper-Matrix, an immersive media space designed by the Seoul-based firm Jonpasang. Dubbed a "kinetic landscape installation," Hyper-Matrix was constructed as the main demonstration hall within the Hyundai Motor Group Exhibition Pavilion at the 2012 Expo in Yeosu, South Korea.[32]

Hyper-Matrix is a three-sided installation of near-seamless white surfaces composed of thousands of 12.5-by-12.5-inch (320 by 320 mm) foam cubes. Mounted on a large, invisible steel frame, the cubes are all independently moveable: individual stepper motors trigger actuators attached to the cubes, allowing them to be shifted back and forth along the z-axis. Not only does this "lo-fi" monochromatic field enable the formation of a virtually limitless variety of words and images, but the near jointless surface—with less than one-quarter inch (5 mm) of space between blocks—is also conducive for front-projection of additional information.

When a visitor first enters the Hyper-Matrix, he or she is confronted with seemingly innocuous white walls. Once the walls come to life, they frame a huge pixelated space in which individual bits of physical matter shift quickly in and out of wall surfaces according to preconfigured animations. As the walls undulate, digital content is selectively projected onto the surfaces in coordination with their movements.

Although the foam pixel bricks of Hyper-Matrix are confined to an enclosed, climate-regulated space, this innovative bridging of electronic and physical realms suggests many future architectural opportunities, including dynamic walls that reconfigure themselves to convey important information, supply temporary seating or storage, or provide targeted shading based on tracking sun angles. Unlike conventional projection screens or electronic displays, the Hyper-Matrix makes the virtual physical, with moving pixels transformed into dancing bricks that communicate both the language of space and the space of language.

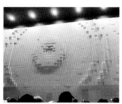

MegaFaces

Sochi, Russia, 2014
Asif Khan

The renowned artist Chuck Close suffers from a bizarre disability called prosopagnosia, otherwise known as face blindness. According to the Prosopagnosia Research Center, face blindness is "an impairment in the recognition of faces," which can lead to significant social problems, given that sufferers often have trouble recognizing family, friends, or even themselves.[33] Close credits his success as a painter of giant portraits to his lifelong attempt to wrestle with this disability, creating larger-than-life paintings of loved ones in order to make a permanent, detailed record of the landscapes of their faces:

The way I work is to make this kind of Brobdingnagian world in which I make the face into a landscape, and I journey across that landscape like Gulliver's Lilliputians, crawling over the face of a giant—not knowing that they were on the face of a giant, but knowing everything about that face. And then what I do is I put all that information together…and I can commit it to memory.[34]

The human face may be considered a window to thought. According to Roman philosopher Cicero, "the countenance is the reflection of the soul."[35] As highly evolved creatures, we are imparted the capability to read faces with remarkable skill, rapidly processing some three thousand potential facial expressions into an interpretation of an individual's mood and intent.[36] Physiognomy, or the practice of face reading, has been studied since the time of Aristotle, and has been actively integrated into a variety of fields such as theater and forensics science.

For the 2014 Sochi Olympic Games, architect Asif Khan created his own larger-than-life celebration of the human face. For his design of a pavilion sponsored by MegaFon, one of Russia's largest telecommunications companies, Khan proposed a kinetic envelope that would replicate the faces of Olympics visitors in three dimensions, at the Brobdingnagian scale of 26 feet (8 m) in height—a 3,500 percent enlargement. Like Jonpasang's Hyper-Matrix, the MegaFaces project employs thousands of actuators that extend and contract to form physical projections, in this case manifesting the topographies of three-dimensional face scans. LED lights incorporated at the end of each of the 11,000 actuators enable accurate and swift individual control and position reporting of the actuators, providing more than 170,000 visitors the uncanny experience of projecting their magnified countenances into space.

The MegaFaces project exhibits a similar aspiration as the work of Chuck Close: to read the detailed landscape of the human face and represent it at a massive scale. Although MegaFaces employs the latest technologies to achieve its effect, this goal is anything but new. From caryatid columns to Mount Rushmore, humanity has frequently projected its image onto the landscape—and the human physiognomy, with its unparalleled expressive potential, makes a potent vehicle for communication within the physical environment. MegaFaces is perhaps the first example to democratize such self-projection, creating a highly accessible bridge between the human face and the architectural facade.

Skin

Lisbon, Portugal, 2010
P-06 Atelier and João Luís Carrilho da Graça

Human language has evolved endlessly over the history of our noosphere, from pictograms on cave walls to Eastern and Western spoken languages to sign language, braille, graphic forms of communication, and even mathematical language. Our newest forms of language arise from the field of computation. ASCII, which stands for American Standard Code for Information Interchange, is a computer industry standard that assigns letters, numbers, and other characters within the 256 slots available in 8-bit code. In other words, it helps translate between human and computational language.

Designed as a multipurpose room in the Knowledge Pavilion, a science and economy museum in Lisbon, Skin was themed around the ASCII standard. The architecture firm P-06 Atelier, in collaboration with architect João Luís Carrilho da Graça, intended for the thin surface lining the interior of the pavilion to reflect the museum's vision of open public information exchange. Characters of various size and area provide apertures in the skin and produce differences in light porosity, visibility, and acoustic properties. By reconfiguring the walls, sound and light can be dynamically and differently filtered from day to day and program to program. Strategically located LED lighting between the outer walls of the building and its ASCII liner create a uniform field of light throughout the space, keeping attention focused on interior exhibitions.

Skin makes information spatial. Language, the often invisible embodiment of human thought, is rendered visible, even viscous and tangible. The characters of the language itself project a vision of the building's users that is much more than merely letters and words applied to a surface. Rather, it is language made phenomenal through its impact on the very materials that produce memorable architecture: light and sound.

Acknowledgments

We would like to express our gratitude to the many individuals who inspired the contents of this book and supported its realization. The seeds of the conceptual premise were planted in 2005, when Marc established the first biomimicry studio at the University of Minnesota School of Architecture—in consultation with Dayna Baumeister and Janine Benyus from the Biomimicry Guild and John Carmody from the Center for Sustainable Building Research—and Blaine had the opportunity to write about lifelike emergent materials for publications like *Architectural Record* and *Popular Science*. After a decade of development, Marc's biomimicry studio has benefited greatly from the generative ideas and tireless efforts of students, as well as collaborating faculty members Lucy Dunne, Vince James, Mithat Konar, Don Luce, Gordon Murdock, Neil Olszewski, Emilie Snell-Rood, and Diane Willow. In 2012 his studio work was exhibited at the Weisman Art Museum at the University of Minnesota in an exhibition called Contextual Flux. For the creative approach to the conception and development of this innovative, process-focused exhibit, Marc is indebted to the Target Studio director and public art curator, Craig Amundsen, and guest curator for the Target Studio for Creative Collaboration, Matthew Groshek.

We would like to thank the organizers and collaborators of several influential conferences in which one or both of us had the opportunity to participate: Ana Fernández de la Mora, Maria Güell, Margarita Kichner, and Jose Luis De Vicente at the Arquinfad symposium "Working With Nature" in Barcelona, 2007; Billie Faircloth, Andrew Kudless, Kiel Moe, and Neri Oxman at the ACADIA national conference "Silicon and Skin" at the University of Minnesota, 2008; and Joanna Aizenberg, Chuck Hoberman, Don Ingber, Jeanne Marie Nisbet, and Jermaine Nicole Reid at the Wyss Institute "Adaptive Architecture Workshop" at Harvard University, 2011. We would also like to thank the visionary editors at *Architect* magazine who have supported the publication of our research since 2006: Braulio Agnese, Hallie Busta, Kriston Capps, Ned Cramer, Katie Gerfen, Sara Johnson, Wanda Lau, Greig O'Brien, Alexandra Rice, Lindsey Roberts, and Katie Weeks.

After deciding to coauthor a book, we received a tremendous amount of help from several key individuals and organizations. We are deeply indebted to Blair Satterfield of the University of British Columbia for his masterful illustrations that appear at the beginning of each chapter. These formidable collections of drawings reveal not only his consummate skill but also his thorough understanding of the natural phenomena and design methods at work. We are grateful to Leslie Van Duzer, director of the University of British Columbia School of Architecture and Landscape Architecture, for her support of Blair's involvement in the project. We would also like to thank Michael Weinstock of the Architectural Association for his insightful foreword to the book. We have been deeply humbled and inspired by Michael's brilliant leadership in the field of emergent technology and design, and his adroit framing of the essential aims of the book provides a compelling picture of the future possibilities in architecture.

We also deeply value the contributions of our project assistants. University of Minnesota architecture students Megan Freeman and David Johansson spent many hours conducting literature and project surveys, as well as helping us craft the overall organizational structure of the book, while Sangyong Hahn and Hwan Kim provided much-needed assistance in deciphering Mass Studies' mystifying Korean Pavilion. University of British Columbia student Catherine He assisted Blair in preparing project illustrations for the "Geosphere," "Hydrosphere," and "Microbial Biosphere" chapters, while vocal expert Tracy Satterfield helped with phonation and vocal physiology for the Korean Pavilion diagram. We are thankful to both institutions for supporting student research assistantships, and we are also grateful to Renee Cheng and Thomas Fisher at the University of Minnesota for supporting Blaine's 2013 sabbatical to work on the book.

We would like to thank Princeton Architectural Press for providing this wonderful publication opportunity, and specifically Meredith Baber, Benjamin English, Jennifer Lippert, Kevin Lippert, and Marielle Suba for being first-rate, tireless collaborators.

Most importantly, we extend our heartfelt gratitude to our families—Heather, Blaine, and Davis Brownell, and Connie, Maeve, and Enna Swackhamer—for their loving support of our work.

Notes

Introduction

1. A concise definition of sustainable is "conserving an ecological balance by avoiding depletion of natural resources." *Oxford English Dictionary Online*, http://www.oxforddictionaries.com/us/definition/american_english/sustainable. Biophilia is defined as "an innate and genetically determined affinity of human beings with the natural world," as established by the biologist E. O. Wilson. *Oxford English Dictionary Online*, http://www.oxforddictionaries.com/us/definition/american_english/biophilia?q=biophilia. Biomimicry is defined as "the design and production of materials, structures, and systems that are modeled on biological entities and processes." *Oxford English Dictionary Online*, http://www.oxforddictionaries.com/us/definition/american_english/biomimicry.

2. Samuel Butler, "Darwin among the Machines," letter to the editor of the *Press*, June 13, 1863.

3. Kevin Kelly, *Out of Control: The New Biology of Machines, Social Systems, and the Economic World* (New York: Basic Books, 1994).

4. W. Brian Arthur, *The Nature of Technology: What It Is and How It Evolves* (New York: Free Press, 2009).

5. Kevin Kelly, *What Technology Wants* (New York: Viking, 2010), 104.

6. A definition of technology is "the application of scientific knowledge for practical purposes, especially in industry." *OxfordDictionaries.com*, http://www.oxforddictionaries.com/us/definition/american_english/technology?q=technology. A definition of design is "the art or action of conceiving of and producing a plan or drawing." *Oxford English Dictionary Online*, http://www.oxforddictionaries.com/us/definition/american_english/design.

7. Karim Rashid, "Karimanifesto," http://www.karimrashid.com/manifesto_fr.html.

8. Koert Van Mensvoort and Hendrik-Jan Grievink, *Next Nature* (Barcelona: Actar, 2012), 124.

9. According to architectural historian Kimberly Elman, organic architecture may be defined as "a reinterpretation of nature's principles as they had been filtered through the intelligent minds of men and women who could then build forms, which are more natural than nature itself." PBS, http://www.pbs.org/flw/legacy/essay1.html.

10. According to geologist Michael Flaxman, geodesign is "a design and planning method, which tightly couples the creation of design proposals with impact simulations informed by geographic contexts." Michael Flaxman, "Geodesign: Fundamental Principles and Routes Forward," lecture at GeoDesign Summit 2010. We propose an expanded definition of geodesign to describe the act of designing in direct relation to the geosphere. In this way, it more closely parallels the concept of biodesign, in which design is executed in direct relation to the functions and processes of living organisms. A definition for bioengineering is the "biological or medical application of engineering principles or engineering equipment." *Merriam Webster*, http://www.merriam-webster.com/dictionary/bioengineering.

Geosphere

1. "How do crystals form and how do they grow?" Kiwi Web, Chemistry & New Zealand, http://www.chemistry.co.nz/crystals_forming.htm.

2. Graeme McMillan, "Grow Your Own Furniture," io9, February 11, 2009, http://io9.com/5151021/grow-your-own-furniture.

3. Ahmet R. Mermut and Angel Faz Cano, "Baseline Studies of the Clay Minerals Society Source Clays: Chemical Analyses of Major Elements," *Clay and Clay Minerals* 49, no. 5 (2001): 381. http://www.clays.org/SOURCE%20CLAYS/sc-ccm/381.pdf.

4. Philip Cohen, "Clay's Matchmaking Could Have Sparked Life," *New Scientist*, October 23, 2003, http://www.newscientist.com/article/dn4307-clays-matchmaking-could-have-sparked-life.html.

5. Manuel De Landa, *A Thousand Years of Nonlinear History* (New York: Swerve Editions, 2000), 26–27.

6. Ibid., 27.

7. Ibid., 28.

8. Ralph L. Dawes and Cheryl D. Dawes, "Geology of the Pacific Northwest: Basics—Rocks and Minerals," Wenatchee Valley College, 2001, http://commons.wvc.edu/rdawes/basics/rocktypes.html.

9. "The Story of Graphene," University of Manchester, http://www.graphene.manchester.ac.uk/story/.

10. Mike Williams, "Carbon's New Champion," *Rice University News*, October 9, 2013, http://news.rice.edu/2013/10/09/carbons-new-champion/.

11. "World Record: Scientists from Northern Germany Produce the Lightest Material in the World," Kiel University, July 17, 2012, http://www.uni-kiel.de/aktuell/pm/2012/2012-212-aerographit-e.shtml; For MWCNT aerogel, see Blaine Brownell, "Strong as Air," *Architect* (April 2011): 56.

12. "Multidisciplinary Team of Researchers Develop World's Lightest Material," *UC Irvine Today*, November 17, 2011, http://today.uci.edu/news/2011/11/nr_lightmetal_111117.php.

13. "Southampton Scientist Develops Strongest, Lightest Glass Nanofibres in the World," University of Southampton, January 10, 2013, http://www.southampton.ac.uk/mediacentre/news/2013/jan/13_05.shtml.

14. "Hard or Soft: at the Touch of a Button New Nanomaterial Switches Properties as Required," Helmholtz Center Geesthacht, June 2, 2011, http://www.hzg.de/public_relations/press_releases/011808/index_0011808.html.en; Mike Williams, "Silicone Liquid Crystal Stiffens with Repeated Compression," *Rice News*, April 29, 2013, http://news.rice.edu/2013/04/29/silicone-liquid-crystal-stiffens-with-repeated-compression-2/.

15. Lynn Yarris, "New Glass Tops Steel in Strength and Toughness," *Lawrence Berkeley National Laboratory News Center*, January 10, 2011, http://newscenter.lbl.gov/news-releases/2011/01/10/new-glass-tops-steel/.

16. "Transparent Conductive Material Could Lead to Power-Generating Windows," *Brookhaven National Laboratory Newsroom*, November 3, 2010, http://www.bnl.gov/newsroom/news.php?a=11195; Jennifer Marcus, "UCLA Researchers Create Highly Transparent Solar Cells for Windows that Generate Electricity," *UCLA Newsroom*, July 20, 2012, http://newsroom.ucla.edu/releases/ucla-researchers-create-highly-236698.

17. "Will 2-D Tin Be the Next Super Material?," SLAC National Accelerator Laboratory, Stanford University, November 21, 2013, https://www6.slac.stanford.edu/news/2013-11-21-tin-super-material-stanene.aspx; "A Folding Ceramic," Max-Planck Gesellschaft, March 27, 2013, http://www.mpg.de/7064293/vanadium-pentoxide-ceramic-paper; "Elastic Electronics: Stretchable Gold Conductor Grows Its Own Wires," *Michigan News*, July 17, 2013, http://www.ns.umich.edu/new/multimedia/videos/21586-elastic-electronics-stretchable-gold-conductor-grows-its-own-wires.

18. Michael Ashby, *Materials and the Environment* (Oxford: Butterworth-Heinemann, 2009), 7.

19. Robin Dennell and Martin Porr, *Southern Asia, Australia, and the Search for Human Origins* (Cambridge: Cambridge University Press, 2014), 2, 77.

20. Mark Hattersley, "The 3D Printer That Can Build a House in 24 Hours," *MSN Innovation*, November 20, 2013,

http://innovation.uk.msn.com/design/the-3d-printer-that-can-build-a-house-in-24-hours.

21. Jeff Blagdon, "British Company Uses 3D Printing to Make Stone Buildings out of Sand," *Verge*, February 21, 2012, http://www.theverge.com/2012/2/21/2811146/3d-printing-d-shape-monolite-enrico-dini.

22. Stone Spray Project, http://www.stonespray.com.

23. "Building Bytes," Design Lab Workshop, http://designlabworkshop.com/introducing-building-bytes/; "Solar Sinter," Markus Kayser, http://www.markuskayser.com/work/solarsinter/.

24. Marcia Goodrich, "Michigan Tech Researcher Using Nanoclays to Build Better Asphalt," *Michigan Tech News*, April 23, 2014, http://www.mtu.edu/news/stories/2012/may/story67607.html.

25. Victor C. Li and Tetsushi Kanda, "Engineered Cementitious Composites for Structural Applications," University of Michigan, http://deepblue.lib.umich.edu/bitstream/handle/2027.42/84890/asceforum_98.pdf.

26. "First Drafts: Primitives," *Atlantic*, http://www.theatlantic.com/sponsored/cadillac-architect-duo/.

27. "Research in Responsive Origami Design Methods Granted $2M by National Science Foundation," *Penn State News & Events*, August 22, 2012, http://www.mne.psu.edu/news/news_detail.cfm?nid=318.

28. Salvatore Benfratello, Giovanna Caiozzo, Marta D'Avenia, and Luigi Palizzolo, "Tradition and Modernity of Catalan Vaults: Historical and Structural Analysis," *Meccanica dei Materiali e delle Strutture* 3, no. 5 (2012): 45–46.

29. See the Block Research Group, ETH Zurich Institute for Technology in Architecture, http://block.arch.ethz.ch/brg/.

30. Birute Saldukiene, *Encyclopedia Lituanica*, vol. 1, ed. Simas Suziedelis, (Boston: Juozas Kapocius, 1970), 85–87.

31. "Chalcanthite," The RRUFF Project, University of Arizona, http://rruff.info/doclib/hom/chalcanthite.pdf.

Atmosphere

1. Reyner Banham, "A Home Is Not a House," *Art in America* 2 (1965): 70.

2. RVTR, "The Stratus Project," www.rvtr.com/research/research-b/.

3. David Kaniewski et al., "Environmental Roots of the Late Bronze Age Crisis," *PLOS ONE* 8, no. 8 (August 14, 2013), doi:10.1371/journal.pone.0071004.

4. Reyner Banham, *The Architecture of the Well-Tempered Environment* (Chicago: University of Chicago Press, 1969), 187.

5. James Calm, "Emissions and Environmental Impacts from Air-Conditioning and Refrigeration Systems," *International Journal of Refrigeration* 25, no. 3 (May 2002): 293.

6. Joe Rao, "Weather Fronts: Definitions and Facts," Live Science, 2003, www.livescience.com/39004-weather-fronts-definitions-facts.html.

7. Mark Pauline, Manuel De Landa, and Mark Dery, "Out of Control," *Survival Research Laboratories,* 1995, srl.org/interviews/out.of.control.html.

8. Martic Chaplin, "Water Absorption Spectrum," Water Structure and Science, April 5, 2014, www1.lsbu.ac.uk/water/vibrat.html.

9. Peter R. Mills, Susannah C. Tomkins, and Luc J. M. Schlangen, "The Effect of High Correlated Colour Temperature Office Lighting on Employee Wellbeing and Work Performance," *Journal of Circadian Rhythms* 5, no. 2 (2007), http://www.jcircadianrhythms.com/content/5/1/2.

10. "Feel-Good Glass for Windows," *Fraunhofer Institute Research News*, July 2, 2012, http://www.fraunhofer.de/en/press/research-news/2012/july/feel-good-glass-for-windows.html.

11. Katie Neal, "Media Advisory: Goodbye, Fluorescent Light Bulbs! See Your Office in a New Light," *Wake Forest University News Center*, December 3, 2012, http://news.wfu.edu/2012/12/03/media-advisory-goodbye-fluorescent-light-bulbs-see-your-office-in-a-new-light/.

12. Heather Clancy, "Freeaire Applies 'Polar Power' to Refrigeration," *ZDNet*, January 4, 2012, http://www.zdnet.com/blog/green/freeaire-applies-polar-power-to-refrigeration/19926.

13. FogScreen, http://www.fogscreen.com; Oliver Wainwright, "Rollup for the Nebula 12, a Wifi Lamp That Brings the Weather Indoors," *The Guardian*, November 29, 2012, http://www.theguardian.com/artanddesign/architecture-design-blog/2012/nov/29/nebula-12-lamp-weather-design.

14. "Solar Ivy," SMIT website, http://www.s-m-i-t.com/#grow_target.

15. Anne Ju, "Students Harness Vibrations from Wind for Electricity," *Cornell Chronicle*, May 25, 2010, http://www.news.cornell.edu/stories/2010/05/researchers-harness-energy-wind-vibrations.

16. William R. Cotton, "Weather Modification by Cloud Seeding: A Status Report 1989–1997," Colorado State University, http://rams.atmos.colostate.edu/gkss.html.

17. See the North American Weather Modification Council website, http://www.nawmc.org.

18. Peter Zumthor, *Atmospheres* (Basel: Birkhäuser, 2006), 13.

19. Arata Isozaki, *Japan-ness in Architecture*, trans. Sabu Kohso (Cambridge, MA: MIT Press, 2006), 151.

20. Japanese historian and architect Terunobu Fujimori coined the term *white school* to describe contemporary Japanese architecture that is characterized by "lightness, elegance, and abstraction." See Blaine Brownell, *Matter in the Floating World: Conversations with Leading Japanese Architects and Designers* (New York: Princeton Architectural Press, 2011), 14.

21. Christo, quoted on ChristoJeanneclaude.net: "When experienced from the inside, that space is almost like a 90-meter-high cathedral." http://www.christojeanneclaude.net/mobile/posts?p=big-air-package.

22. "The Cloud Pavilion by Schmidt Hammer Lassen Architects Opens at Shanghai West Bund Biennial," *Bustler*, October 28, 2013, http://www.bustler.net/index.php/article/the_cloud_pavilion_by_schmidt_hammer_lassen_architects_opens_at_shanghai_we/.

23. "Schmidt Hammer Installs Pavilions at Shanghai West Bund Biennial," World Construction Network, October 28, 2013, http://www.worldconstructionnetwork.com/news/schmidt-hammer-installs-pavilions-at-shanghai-west-bund-biennial-281013/.

24. David Streit, "Gardening in Another Dimension: 'Nanoclimate,'" *Washington Post*, May 5, 2011, http://www.washingtonpost.com/blogs/capital-weather-gang/post/gardening-in-another-dimension-nanoclimate/2011/05/05/AF0CSKyF_blog.html.

25. Robert Greenler, *Rainbows, Halos, and Glories* (Cambridge: Cambridge University Press, 1980), 69.

26. Kyle Vanhemert, "Under the Miami Sun, a Glistening Palace Made of Crystals," *Fast Company*, December 6, 2012, http://www.fastcodesign.com/1671392/under-the-miami-sun-a-glistening-palace-made-of-crystals#2.

27. Parhelia by Asif Khan, *Dezeen Magazine*, December 8, 2012, http://www.dezeen.com/2012/12/08/parhelia-ice-halo-installation-by-asif-khan/.

28. Mark Elling Rosheim, *Leonardo's Lost Robots* (New York: Springer, 2006), 115.

29. Julian Guthrie, "Charles Sowers Creates 'Windswept' for S.F Museum," *SFGate*, February 21, 2012, http://www.sfgate.com/art/article/Charles-Sowers-creates-Windswept-for-S-F-museum-3344743.php.

Hydrosphere

1. Gottfried Semper, *The Four Elements of Architecture* (New York: Cambridge University Press, 2011).

2. According to policy expert Brahma Chellaney, water "remains a greatly underappreciated and underpriced resource despite being central to life." See Brahma Chellaney, *Water, Peace, and War: Confronting the Global Water Crisis* (Lanham, MD: Rowman & Littlefield, 2013), 277.

3. Joachim Radkau, *Nature and Power: A Global History of the Environment* (Cambridge: Cambridge University Press, 2008), 93.

4. Pierre-Louis Viollet, *Water Engineering in Ancient Civilizations: 5,000 Years of History* (Boca Raton, FL: CRC Press, 2007), 16; Rodney Castleden, *Minoans* (London: Routledge, 2002), 189.

5. Lance Frazer, "Paving Paradise: The Peril of Impervious Surfaces," *Environmental Health Perspectives* 113, no. 7 (July 2005): A456–A462.

6. Randy Fertel, "The Mississippi River Delta Must Be Restored," *New York Times*, January 27, 2012, http://www.nytimes.com/2012/01/28/opinion/the-mississippi-river-delta-must-be-restored.html.

7. R. Nave, "The Hydrologic Cycle," Hyperphysics, Department of Physics and Astronomy, Georgia State University, http://hyperphysics.phy-astr.gsu.edu/hbase/chemical/hydcyc.html.

8. Rusty L. Meyer, *The Basics of Physics* (Westport, CT: Greenwood Press, 2006), 86.

9. R. Nave, "Dipole Moment of Water," Hyperphysics, Department of Physics and Astronomy, Georgia State University, http://hyperphysics.phy-astr.gsu.edu/hbase/electric/diph2o.html.

10. "Why is Water a Liquid at Room Temperature?" *Stoichiometric Equivalent*, November 14, 2010, http://stoichiometricequiv.blogspot.com/2010/11/why-is-water-liquid-at-room-temperature.html.

11. Paul R. Josephson, *Industrialized Nature* (Washington, D.C.: Island Press, 2002), 48.

12. Matti Kummu, Philip J. Ward, Hans de Moel, and Olli Varis, "Is Physical Water Scarcity a New Phenomenon? Global Assessment of Water Shortage over the Last Two Millennia," *Environmental Research Letters* 5 (July–September 2010), doi:10.1088/1748-9326/5/3/034006, http://iopscience.iop.org/1748-9326/5/3/034006/fulltext/.

13. Ian Tucker, "Edward Linacre: It's Possible to Get Water from Thin Air," *Guardian*, November 19, 2011, http://www.theguardian.com/technology/2011/nov/20/edward-linacre-airdrop-bright-idea.

14. Blaine Brownell, "Watercone," in *Transmaterial: A Catalog of Materials That Redefine Our Physical Environment*, ed. Blaine Brownell (New York: Princeton Architectural Press, 2006), 136; Blaine Brownell, "Solar Water Tarp," in *Transmaterial 3: A Catalog of Materials That Redefine Our Physical Environment*, ed. Blaine Brownell (New York: Princeton Architectural Press, 2010), 126; "Life Straw: Drink What You Want, When You Want," *Examiner*, February 6, 2013, http://www.examiner.com/article/life-straw-drink-what-you-want-when-you-want-1.

15. Hannah Hickey, "Students Water-Testing Tool Wins $40,000, Launches Nonprofit," University of Washington, December 20, 2010, http://www.washington.edu/news/2010/12/20/students-water-testing-tool-wins-40000-launches-nonprofit/; Brownell, "River Glow," *Transmaterial 3*, 231.

16. WorldWater & Solar Technologies website, http://www.worldwatersolar.com.

17. "Hydroelectric Lamp," Hierve website, http://www.en.hierve.com/projects/hydroelectric-lamp/.

18. "Tunable Material," Wyss Institute website, http://wyss.harvard.edu/viewpage/422/.

19. "Tuteja Group Develops Superomniphobic Surfaces," University of Michigan Materials Science and Engineering, http://www.mse.engin.umich.edu/about/news/tuteja-group-develops-superomniphobic-surfaces; "Nano-Cone Textures Generate Extremely 'Robust' Water-Repellent Surfaces," *Brookhaven National Laboratory Newsroom*, October 21, 2013, http://www.bnl.gov/newsroom/news.php?a=11583.

20. Brownell, "Lotusan," *Transmaterial 1*, 170; Blaine Brownell, "Activ," in *Transmaterial 2: A Catalog of Materials That Redefine Our Physical Environment*, ed. Blaine Brownell (New York: Princeton Architectural Press, 2008), 135.

21. "Cotton with Special Coating Collects Water from Fogs in Desert," Eindhoven University of Technology, January 21, 2013, http://www.tue.nl/en/university/news-and-press/news/cotton-with-special-coating-collects-water-from-fogs-in-desert/.

22. Meryle Secrest, *Frank Lloyd Wright: A Biography* (Chicago: University of Chicago Press, 1998), 479.

23. Zygmunt Bauman, *Liquid Modernity* (Cambridge: Polity, 2000).

24. Brownell, *Matter in the Floating World*, 198.

25. "Blob Motility II—Colony," Metamorphic Architecture, Akira Wakita Laboratory, Keio University, 2011, http://metamo.sfc.keio.ac.jp/project/colony/index.html.

26. "B-surfaces," B. lab Italia, http://blabitalia.com/en/products/b-surfaces/watercolor/.

27. Brownell, "Wet Lamp," *Transmaterial 2*, 212; Brownell, "Watercolors," *Transmaterial 3*, 134; Brownell, "Water Logo," *Matter in the Floating World*, 97; Brownell, "SmartFountain," *Transmaterial 2*, 234; Solid Poetry website, http://solidpoetry.com.

28. "British Pavilion Expo," Grimshaw, http://grimshaw-architects.com/project/british-pavilion-expo/.

29. Hungarian Pavilion: "Jobb város, jobb élet—magyar pavilon a sanghaji expón egy építész szemével," October 13, 2010, http://epiteszforum.hu/jobb-varos-jobb-elet-magyar-pavilon-a-sanghaji-expon-egy-epitesz-szemevel; University of Arizona Solar Decathlon House, "Solar Decathlon 2009," http://www.solardecathlon.gov/past/2009/team_arizona.html.

30. Guy Nordenson, Catherine Seavitt, Adam Yarinsky, *On the Water: Palisade Bay* (New York: Museum of Modern Art, 2010); Sarah McKenzie, "RiverFirst Group Reveals Design Ideas, Fundraising Strategies," *Journal*, May 3, 2013, http://www.journalmpls.com/news-feed/riverfirst-group-reveals-design-ideas-fundraising-strategies.

31. Rachel Pepling, "Soap Bubbles," *Chemical & Engineering News* 81, no. 17 (April 28, 2003): 34, http://pubs.acs.org/cen/whatstuff/stuff/8117sci3.html.

32. Tom Garrison, *Oceanography: An Invitation to Marine Science* (Independence, KY: Cengage Learning, 2012), 311.

33. Mari N. Jensen, "The Platonic Form of Stalactites," *UANews*, December 2, 2004, http://uanews.org/story/platonic-form-stalactites.

34. Ibid.

Microbial Biosphere

1. "Microbial Home," *Philips*, October 19, 2011, http://www.design.philips.com/about/design/designportfolio/design_futures/microbial_home.page.

2. "Philips Launches 'Microbial Home' New Forward Looking Design Concepts," *Philips*, October 20, 2011, http://www.newscenter.philips.com/main/design/news/press/2011/philips_launches%20_microbial_home_new_forward_looking_design_concepts.wpd.

3. "What Is an Extremophile?" Science Education Resource Center, Carleton College, http://serc.carleton.edu/microbelife/extreme/extremophiles.html.

4. Alma Smith Payne, *The Cleere Observer: A Biography of Antoni Van Leeuwenhoek* (London: Macmillan, 1970), 13.

5. According to the Baylor College of Medicine, "Infectious diseases are the second leading cause of death worldwide, after heart disease, and are responsible for more deaths annually than cancer." See "Infectious Diseases," Baylor College of Medicine, https://www.bcm.edu/departments/molecular-virology-and-microbiology/id.

6. Peter Vinten-Johansen et al., *Cholera, Chloroform, and the Science of Medicine: A Life of John Snow* (Oxford: Oxford University Press, 2003), 395.

7. With his discovery of the anthrax bacterium in 1876, bacteriologist Robert Koch played an essential role in refuting the miasma theory. "Robert Koch, 1843–1910," Harvard University Library, http://ocp.hul.harvard.edu/contagion/koch.html.

8. Michael Pollan, "Some of My Best Friends Are Germs," *New York Times Magazine*, May 15, 2013, http://www.nytimes.com/2013/05/19/magazine/say-hello-to-the-100-trillion-bacteria-that-make-up-your-microbiome.html.

9. Ibid.

10. Howard Gest, "The Discovery of Microorganisms by Robert Hooke and Antoni Van Leeuwenhoek, Fellows of the Royal Society," *Royal Society Journal of the History of Science* 58 (May 22, 2004), 187, http://rsnr.royalsocietypublishing.org/content/58/2/187.full.pdf.

11. Min Alverson, "Boom or Bust? Diatoms Decide," *CNRS International Magazine* (Centre National de la Recherche Scientifique), http://www2.cnrs.fr/en/519.htm.

12. "Joanna Aizenberg, Ph.D," Wyss Institute at Harvard University, http://wyss.harvard.edu/viewpage/118/joanna-aizenberg.

13. Brownell, "Myoaband," *Transmaterial 3*, 81.

14. Blaine Brownell, "Fungus Furniture," *Architect*, August 22, 2013, http://www.architectmagazine.com/furniture/fungus-furniture.aspx.

15. Eric Klarenbeek, http://www.ericklarenbeek.com.

16. Megan Fellman, "Addressing the Nuclear Waste Issue," *Northwestern University News*, April 4, 2011, http://www.northwestern.edu/newscenter/stories/2011/04/algae-nuclear-cleanup.html.

17. "BacillaFilla: Fixing Cracks in Concrete," Team Newcastle, International Genetically Engineered Machine (iGEM) Foundation, 2010, http://2010.igem.org/Team:Newcastle.

18. "Bielefeld Students Take Part in iGEM Competition," *Uni.news*, University of Bielefeld, http://ekvv.uni-bielefeld.de/blog/uninews/entry/using_bacteria_batteries_to_make.

19. Ibid.

20. Marianne Spoon, "The Next Bright Idea: Microbe-powered 'Biobulb' Earns WID Students Spot in Popular Science Magazine Competition," Wisconsin Institute for Discovery, August 19, 2013, http://wid.wisc.edu/featured-science/the-next-bright-idea-microbe-powered-biobulb-earns-uw-students-spot-in-popular-science-magazine-competition/.

21. "To Programme Architecture," http://thisisalive.com/bio-computation/.

22. "Installation: Museum of Arts and Design," Diller Scofidio + Renfro, http://www.dsrny.com/#/projects/art-of-scent.

23. "Algal Oil Biodiesel," *Analysis of Innovative Feedstock Sources and Production Technologies for Renewable Fuels*, University of Texas at Austin report for the Environmental Protection Agency XA-83379501-0, 6-3, http://www.utexas.edu/research/ceer/biofuel/pdf/Report/h_EPA%20Alt%20Fuels%20Final%20Report_Chapter%206_Final.pdf.

24. "The Interaction of Biological Materials with Geotechnical Processes Has Long Been Ignored by Geotechnical Engineering, and Its Importance is Just Beginning to be Realized," University of California, Davis, Soil Interactions Laboratory, http://www.sil.ucdavis.edu/biosoil-overview.htm.

25. "Dune," Magnus Larsson, http://www.magnuslarsson.com/architecture/dune.asp.

26. Jannis Hülsen, "Xylinum Cones," October 2013, http://www.jannishuelsen.com/?/work/Xylinumcones/.

27. Ibid.

Botanical Biosphere

1. Matt Davis, "Cattedrale Vegetale, Giuliano Mauri," *ARCH2O*, http://www.arch2o.com/cattedrale-vegetale-giuliano-mauri/.

2. Reyner Banham, *The Architecture of the Well-Tempered Environment* (Chicago: University of Chicago Press, 1969), 19.

3. Luis-Fernández Galiano, *Fire and Memory: On Architecture and Energy* (Cambridge, MA: MIT Press, 2000), 8.

4. Charles Eisen, frontispiece in Marc-Antoine Laugier, *Essai sur l'architecture* (Paris: Chez Duchesne,1755).

5. Gottfried Semper, *The Four Elements of Architecture and Other Writings*, trans. Harry Francis Mallgrave and Wolfgang Hermann (Cambridge: Cambridge University Press, 1851), 103.

6. Paul R. Josephson, *Industrialized Nature* (Washington, D.C.: Island Press, 2002), 70.

7. David Morris, "The Once and Future Carbohydrate Economy," *American Prospect*, March 20, 2006, http://prospect.org/article/once-and-future-carbohydrate-economy.

8. Blaine Brownell, "Stadthaus," in *Material Strategies: Innovative Applications in Architecture* (New York: Princeton Architectural Press, 2012), 70; Wood Innovation and Design Centre (WIDC) website, http://www.woodfirstbc.ca/projects/wood-innovation-and-design-centre.

9. "Nanocellulose Pilot Plant to Be Unveiled at Forest Products Lab," *USDA Forest Products Laboratory*, July 16, 2012, http://www.fpl.fs.fed.us/news/newsreleases/releases/20120716.shtml.

10. Blaine Brownell, "Aerocork," *Architect*, July 11, 2010, http://www.architectmagazine.com/blogs/postdetails.aspx?BlogId=mindmatterblog&postId=96226.

11. "Seaweed under the Roof," *Fraunhofer Institute Research News*, March 1, 2013, http://www.fraunhofer.de/en/press/research-news/2013/march/seaweed-under-the-roof.html; "Tofu Ingredient Yields Formaldehyde Free Glue for Plywood and Other Wood Products," *American Chemical Society News Service*, August 25, 2010, https://www.acs.org/content/acs/en/pressroom/presspacs/2010/acs-presspac-august-25-2010/tofu-ingredient-yields-formaldehyde-free-glue-for-plywood-and-other-wood-products.html.

12. "Bioplastics: A Global Market Watch, 2011–2016," *Research and Markets*, December 2012, http://www.researchandmarkets.com/research/96d7zk/bioplastics_a.

13. "Film coatings Made from Whey, *Fraunhofer Institute Research News*, January 2, 2012, http://www.fraunhofer.de/en/press/research-news/2012/january/film-coatings-whey.html; Blaine Brownell, "Brazilian Bioplastic as Strong as Kevlar," *Architect*, April 23, 2011, http://www.architectmagazine.com/blogs/postdetails.aspx?BlogId=mindmatterblog&postId=103019; "Dandelion Rubber," *Fraunhofer Institute Research News*, September 1, 2009, http://www.fraunhofer.de/en/press/research-news/2009/09/

Dandelionrubber.html; Blaine Brownell, "Scientists Develop Bio-Based Resins for Building Construction," *Architect*, April 2, 2011, http://www.architectmagazine.com/blogs/postdetails.aspx?BlogId=mindmatterblog&PostId=102448.

14. Michael Wolf, "3-D Printing with Paper at Your Local Office Supply Store? Yep, If Mcor Has Its Way," *Forbes*, March 13, 2013, http://www.forbes.com/sites/michaelwolf/2013/03/13/3d-printing-with-paper-at-your-local-office-supply-store-yep-if-mcor-has-its-way/.

15. Cornell Creative Machines Lab, Cornell University, http://creativemachines.cornell.edu/node/194.

16. Sarah Ostman, "Evolution Inspires More Efficient Solar Cell Design," *News from McCormick,* Northwestern University, January 24, 2013, http://www.mccormick.northwestern.edu/news/articles/2013/01/evolution-inspires-more-efficient-solar-cell-design.html.

17. David L. Chandler, "Solar Cell, Heal Thyself," *MIT News*, September 7, 2010, http://newsoffice.mit.edu/2010/self-healing-solar.

18. "Trees Used to Create Recyclable, Efficient Solar Cell," *Georgia Tech Center for Organic Photonics and Electronics*, March 25, 2013, http://www.cope.gatech.edu/news/release.php?nid=201941.

19. Martha Heil, "A Battery Made of Wood?," *UMN Right Now*, University of Maryland, June 19, 2013, http://www.umdrightnow.umd.edu/news/battery-made-wood; "A Window That Washes Itself? New Nano-material May Revolutionize Solar Panels and Batteries, Too," *Science Daily*, December 4, 2009, http://www.sciencedaily.com/releases/2009/12/091203132159.htm; "Gold Nanoparticles Advance Bioluminescence," *Photonics.com*, November 8, 2010, http://www.photonics.com/Article.aspx?AID=44881.

20. "Active Modular Phytoremediation System," *Case.RPI.edu*, http://www.case.rpi.edu/CASE.html.

21. Brian Merchant, "Living Bridges in India Have Grown for 500 Years," *Treehugger*, September 28, 2010, http://www.treehugger.com/sustainable-product-design/living-bridges-in-india-have-grown-for-500-years-pics.html.

22. "Aldar Central Market," hoberman, http://www.hoberman.com/portfolio/aldarcentralmarket.php?projectname=Aldar+Central+Market.

23. "The Air Flow(er)," liftarchitects, http://www.liftarchitects.com/air-flower/.

24. See "Thermobimetal Strips," Beijing Beiye Functional Materials Corporation, http://www.bygcg.com/product_6.htm.

25. Roger P. Hangarter, "Circadian Responses," Plants-in-Motion, Indiana University, http://plantsinmotion.bio.indiana.edu/plantmotion/movements/leafmovements/clocks.html.

26. Morris Hickey Morgan, *Vitruvius: The Ten Books on Architecture* (Mineola, NY: Dover Publications, 1960).

27. Douglas D. Stokke, Qinglin Wu, and Guangping Han, *Introduction to Wood and Natural Fiber Composites* (Hoboken, NJ: John Wiley & Sons, 2013), 72.

28. Achim Menges, "HygroScope: Meteorosensitive Morphology," http://www.achimmenges.net/?p=5083.

29. Jason Payne, "Raspberry Fields," http://www.hirsuta.com/RASP.html.

Zoological Biosphere
1. Kelly, *Out of Control*.
2. Edward O. Price, *Animal Domestication and Behavior* (Wallingford, UK: CABI, 2002), 1.
3. John Tyler Bonner, *Morphogenesis: An Essay on Development* (New York: Atheneum, 1963).
4. Cliff Tabin, interview by John Rubin, *What Is Evo Devo?*, PBS, January 5, 2009.
5. Ibid.
6. "Zoobotics," *Economist*, July 7, 2011, http://www.economist.com/node/18925855.
7. Ibid.
8. Janna C. Nawroth et al., "A Tissue-Engineered Jellyfish with Biomimetic Propulsion," *Nature Biotechnology* 30 (July 22, 2012), 792–97, http://www.nature.com/nbt/journal/v30/n8/full/nbt.2269.html.
9. Alvin Powell, "As Strong as an Insect's Shell," *Harvard Gazette*, February 2, 2012, http://news.harvard.edu/gazette/story/2012/02/as-strong-as-an-insect's-shell/.
10. Mindy Dulai, "How to Make a Crab Shell See-through," *Royal Society of Chemistry*, November 30, 2011, http://www.rsc.org/chemistryworld/News/2011/November/30111102.asp.
11. Denise Brehm, "Printing Artificial Bone," *MIT News*, June 17, 2003, http://newsoffice.mit.edu/2013/printing-artificial-bone-0617.
12. "Lifelike Cooling for Sunbaked Windows," *Wyss Institute*, July 30, 2013, http://wyss.harvard.edu/viewpressrelease/119/.
13. "Tears? Forget Them!" *SINTEF*, September 16, 2011, http://www.sintef.no/home/Press-Room/Research-News/Tears-Forget-them/.
14. "How a Fish 'Broke' a Law of Physics," *University of Bristol*, October 21, 2012, http://www.bristol.ac.uk/news/2012/8865.html.

15. Rick Kubetz, "Bugs View Inspires New Digital Cameras Unique Imaging Capabilities," *Engineering at Illinois*, April 29, 2013, http://engineering.illinois.edu/news/article/2013-04-29-bugs-view-inspires-new-digital-cameras-unique-imaging-capabilities.

16. "Mapping a Room in a Snap," *EPFL News*, June 18, 2013, http://actu.epfl.ch/news/mapping-a-room-in-a-snap/.

17. Martin Kettle, "Spider Gene Spins Goats' Milk Into Super Fibre," *Guardian*, May 19, 2000, http://www.theguardian.com/world/2000/may/20/martinkettle.

18. Mayumi Negishi, "Can Spider Web Be Replicated? A Japanese Startup Thinks So.," *Wall Street Journal*, July 8, 2013, http://online.wsj.com/news/articles/SB10001424127887324399404578583562603579062.

19. Steve Koppes, "Universal Solvent No Match for New Self-healing Sticky Gel," *University of Chicago News*, January 27, 2011, http://news.uchicago.edu/article/2011/01/27/universal-solvent-no-match-new-self-healing-sticky-gel.

20. "Blood Bricks," Munro Studio website, http://www.munro-studio.com.

21. Qmilk, http://en.qmilk.eu.

22. Andrew Kudless, "Animal Architectures," lecture, California College of the Arts, Oakland, CA, February 2012.

23. Mick Pearce Architect, "Eastgate Development Harare," http://www.mickpearce.com/works/office-public-buildings/eastgate-development-harare/.

24. "Flying Machine Enabled Construction," ETH Zurich, http://www.idsc.ethz.ch/Research_DAndrea/Archives/Flying_Machine_Enabled_Construction.

25. Matt Shipman, "Researchers Develop Technique to Remotely Control Cockroaches," *Abstract*, North Carolina State University, September 5, 2012, http://web.ncsu.edu/abstract/science/wms-cockroach-steering/.

26. "Climate Change and Biodiversity," Harvard School of Public Health, http://chge.med.harvard.edu/topic/climate-change-and-biodiversity-loss.

27. Kyle Mastalinski, "Hive City," July 25, 2012, http://hivecity.wordpress.com/2012/07/25/elevator-b/.

28. "Theme," *Expo 2012*, Yeosu, Korea, http://eng.expo2012.kr/is/ps/unitybbs/bbs/selectBbsDetail.html?ispsBbsId=BBS001&ispsNttId=0000000002.

29. Ensamble Studio, "Truffle," http://www.ensamble.info/actualizacion/projects/truffle.

Noosphere

1. Victor Hugo, *The Hunchback of Notre-Dame*, trans. Walter J. Cobb (New York: Signet, 1964), 174.

2. Mass Studies, "Shanghai Expo 2010: Korea Pavilion," http://www.massstudies.com/projects/expo_txtEN.html.

3. Ibid.

4. Hugo, *The Hunchback of Notre-Dame*, 175.

5. George S. Levit, *Biogeochemistry—Biosphere—Noosphere* (Berlin: VWB-Verlag für Wissenschaft und Bildung, 2001), 80.

6. Ibid., 167.

7. Manuel De Landa, *A Thousand Years of Nonlinear History* (New York: Swerve Editions, 2000), 185.

8. Ibid., 186.

9. Hugo, *The Hunchback of Notre-Dame*, 182.

10. Kenya Hara, *Designing Design* (Baden: Lars Müller Publishers, 2007), 156–57.

11. De Landa, *A Thousand Years of Nonlinear History*, 259.

12. Lewis Thomas, "Living Language," *The Lives of a Cell: Notes of a Biology Watcher* (New York: Penguin, 1974), 106.

13. "Language," def. 1 in *Oxford English Dictionary Online*, http://www.oxforddictionaries.com/us/definition/american_english/language.

14. "Language" def. 2.1 in *Oxford English Dictionary Online*, http://www.oxforddictionaries.com/us/definition/american_english/language.

15. Ferdinand de Saussure, *Course in General Linguistics*, trans. and ann. Roy Harris (London: Duckworth, 1983), 111.

16. Julian Lincoln Simon, *The Ultimate Resource 2* (Princeton, NJ: Princeton University Press, 1996); Kevin Kelly, *What Technology Wants* (New York: Viking, 2010), 93.

17. Kelly, *What Technology Wants*, 14.

18. Brownell, *Transmaterial 3*, 232.

19. Blaine Brownell, "Using Real-Time Climate Data to Drive Design," *Architect*, April 16, 2013, http://www.architectmagazine.com/architecture/using-real-time-climate-data-to-drive-design.aspx.

20. Helen Knight, "New System Uses Low-Power Wi-Fi Signal to Track Moving Humans—Even Behind Walls," *MIT News*, June 28, 2013, http://newsoffice.mit.edu/2013/new-system-uses-low-power-wi-fi-signal-to-track-moving-humans-0628.

21. Bruce Sterling, *Shaping Things* (Cambridge, MA: MIT Press, 2005), 76.

22. IBM Research, "Cognitive Computing," http://www.research.ibm.com/cognitive-computing.

23. Louis Bergeron, "Stanford Researchers Build Transparent, Super-Stretchy Skin-like Sensor," *Stanford News*, October 24, 2011, http://news.stanford.edu/news/2011/october/stretchy-skinlike-sensor-102411.html.

24. Blaine Brownell, "When Our Technology Senses Us," *Architect*, July 5, 2012, http://www.architectmagazine.com/technology/when-our-technology-senses-us.aspx.

25. A. C. C. Rotzetter et al., "Thermoresponsive Polymer Induced Sweating Surfaces as an Efficient Way to Passively Cool Buildings," *Advanced Materials* 24, no. 39 (October 9, 2012), 5352, http://onlinelibrary.wiley.com/doi/10.1002/adma.201202574/abstract.

26. Nancy Spiegel, "The Enlightenment and Grand Library Design," *Humanities & Social Sciences News*, April 26, 2011, http://news.lib.uchicago.edu/blog/2011/04/26/the-enlightenment-and-grand-library-design/.

27. Hugh Westbrook, "How Twitter Has Changed Language," *Wordability*, January 18, 2013, http://wordability.net/2013/01/18/how-twitter-has-changed-language/.

28. "Datagrove/Future Cities Lab," *ArchDaily*, September 25, 2012, http://www.archdaily.com/?p=276041.

29. Angela Suico, "Does 'Rick Rolling' Ring a Bell?," *Inbound Marketing Blog*, May 18, 2013, http://www.inboundmarketingagents.com/inbound-marketing-agents-blog/bid/291110/How-the-Internet-Has-Changed-the-English-Language.

30. Rogers Stirk Harbour + Partners, "Centre Pompidou Masterplan," http://www.richardrogers.co.uk/work/masterplans/centre_pompidou_masterplan.

31. Hugo, *The Hunchback of Notre-Dame*, 175.

32. Jonpasang, "Hyper-Matrix," http://jonpasang.com/?portfolio=hypermatrix.

33. "Research," Prosopagnosia Research Centers at Harvard University and University College London, https://www.faceblind.org/research/index.html.

34. Chuck Close, interviewed by Robert Krulwich, "Strangers in the Mirror," *World Science Festival*, New York, NY, June 2010, http://worldsciencefestival.com/videos/painting_blind.

35. Cicero, quoted in Leslie A. Zebrowitz, *Reading Faces: Window to the Soul?* (Boulder, CO: Westview Press, 1997), 2.

36. James W. Neuliep, *Intercultural Communication: A Contextual Approach* (Thousand Oaks, CA: Sage, 2011), 279.

Image Credits

Project Index

109751